CRESTLINE

100 YEARS OF
SEMI
TRUCKS

Ronald G. Adams

MBI Publishing Company

First published in 2000 by MBI Publishing Company, 729 Prospect Avenue, PO Box 1, Osceola, WI 54020-0001 USA

MBI Publishing Company books are also available at discounts in bulk quantity for industrial or sales-promotional use. For details write to Special Sales Manager at Motorbooks International Wholesalers & Distributors, 729 Prospect Avenue, PO Box 1, Osceola, WI 54020-0001 USA.

Library of Congress Cataloging-in-Publication Data
   100 years of semi trucks / Ronald G. Adams
     p.cm. — (Crestline)
   Includes index.
   ISBN 0-7603-0769-5 (hc:alk. paper)
    1. Trucks—History. I Title. II. Crestline series
   TL230.A32 2000
   629.224'0904—dc21   00-039462

On the front cover: *Photo courtesy Freightliner Corporation*

On the back cover: Back in the mid-1950s, many new trucking companies were getting into the haulage business, including the Long Island Rural Motor Express Co., located in New York City. Truck No. 24 was a Day-Elder five-ton job. The body was 16 feet, 8 inches high. The cab had weather curtains, as did the body. Day-Elder trucks were made from 1918 to 1931 in Newark, New Jersey. *Ron Adams collection*

Edited by Steve Hendrickson
Designed by Arthur Durkee

Printed in China

CONTENTS

DEDICATION

I'd like to dedicate this to my friend Robert "Bob" Parrish of Camden, New Jersey. I first met Robert in the summer of 1965. Over the ensuing years we made many trips in his reliable 1956 Plymouth to visit the truck stops in the Carlisle, Pennsylvania, area as well as the Bartonsville "76" truck stop, where we shot pictures of many interesting trucks. Robert was a nice person and always got very excited when he saw an interesting truck.

Robert had taken a lot of truck shots in the late 1950s in the Camden and Philadelphia areas, and in 1970, I bought a good part of his collection. By the mid the 1970s, Robert's health started failing, and I lost all contact with him. Those nine years of truck photography that we did together left me with a lot of good memories. So, Robert "Bob" Parrish, "This one's for you!"

—Ron Adams

ACKNOWLEDGMENTS

A list of the names of those who made this book possible would be rather lengthy. I'd like to thank the people and companies listed in the photo credits for sending me photographs over the years, as well as those collectors who were willing to trade and exchange negatives and pictures. A few of them have been exchanging and trading with me for over 35 years. Thank you, too, to the sources from whom I have received information for more than 40 years.

Also, thanks to those drivers I've gotten to know over the years for the information they have told me about the companies that they drove for. Putting together all the photographs and information I received is what made this book a reality, so a big thank-you to everyone.

—Ron Adams

4

PREFACE

I've been asked many times, "What got you interested in trucks?" At first, I didn't really have an answer. But then one day, while thinking back to when I was a child, I finally came up with the answer—I guess I can give my father credit for getting me into this hobby. Around 1943, my father's best friend, Newt Bachman, bought the Springside Hotel, located along Route 22 near Allentown, Pennsylvania. Newt and my parents were good friends, and they would visit Newt and his wife Mae at the hotel several times a week. As I grew up, the Springside Hotel seemed like our second home because we were there so often. For my brothers and me, there wasn't much that we could do at the hotel except sit in at the dining room windows and watch the trucks go by. My younger brother, Larry, never took much interest in trucks, but my older brother, Franklin, would like to count how many trucks would go by while we were there. I always liked to see their colors and the names on the trucks. I remember names like Super Service Motor Freight, Speedway Carriers, Continental, Kramer Bros. Freight Lines, Riss, Mason Dixon Lines, Atlantic States Motor Lines, and Travelers Motor Freight, just to name a few.

Then from 1956 to 1959, a new four-lane highway (I-78) was built to take the heavy volume of traffic off the old two-lane Route 22. This new highway took some land from my grandparents' farm. When we would go to visit them, I would walk to the highway and watch the trucks pass by. As a 12-year-old in 1959, I remember wanting to have some pictures of some of these trucks. So I took down names of companies and where they were from, and that night I started writing letters. The first company I wrote to was Associated Transport Co. in New York City. On Monday morning, my letter went out with the 8 A.M. mail. One week later, I got their reply-along with two photographs of one of their trucks (one of which is in chapter five of this book). I followed up with more letters to Transamerican Freight Lines in Detroit, Roadway, Cooper Jarrett, Arrow Carriers, Eazor Express, PIE, Motor Cargo, Kramer Bros., Garrett, Eastern Express, and others. The results were good. In 1961, I received one of my most favorite pictures from Garrett Freightlines of the truck that was used in the TV program "Cannonball." Later, I bought a camera and began taking pictures of trucks myself.

From that first letter in January 1959 up to today, I've had countless hours of enjoyment collecting truck pictures. From January 1966, I've had many days of fun standing along Interstate 78 taking pictures of the trucks as they passed by, which I still do today.

INTRODUCTION

Overland transport is hardly a new thing, with horses and wagons serving to carry things from here to there for centuries. Although the horse and wagon were replaced by the truck in the early 1900s, trucking itself did not become a huge industry until the nation's highway system was established.

Though 100 years covers most of the history of trucks, we've been hauling stuff from one place to another since the beginning of time. In America, the history of hauling begins on the water, where canoes and barges moved freight on rivers and canals. Over land, horse-drawn wagons and stagecoaches moved people and their stuff from east to west and back. Railroads then revolutionized the transportation industry, making it possible to haul more freight and passengers faster and more cheaply than ever.

But the history of trucking really begins with the automobile. By 1900 there were 54 different makes of cars, and thanks in large part to the vision of Henry Ford, within 25 years the car became the personal transportation device of choice for many Americans.

Early trucks were nothing more than an automobile body cut away for cargo space. They weren't very big, but they served the purpose. Before long, trucks had proved they could haul more freight for less money than a freight wagon.

As demand for larger and more versatile trucks grew, manufacturers proliferated: According to the Red Book-Blue Book Autobiography, there were an estimated 1,800 truck manufacturers in the early part of the 20th century. Some of the earlier brand names of trucks were included:

Bessemer (1904)–Chicago, Illinois
Chase (1907)–Syracuse, New York
Davies (1905)–St. Louis, Missouri
Fisher (1900)–Chicago, Illinois
Garford (1902)–Lima, Ohio
Hildebrand (1895)–Chicago, Illinois
Kearns (1908)–Beavertown, Pennsylvania
Mack (1900)–New York, New York
McMullen (1900)–Chicago, Illinois
Overland (1908)–Toledo, Ohio
REO (1908)–Lansing, Michigan

Back in the late 1950s and early 1960s, this GMC truck and Fruehauf trailer starred in "Cannonball," a Sunday night television series. The driver, "Cannonball" Mike Malone, was played by Paul Birch and his co-driver, Jerry Austin, was played by William Campbell. This photo came from Garrett Freightlines in Pocatello, Idaho in 1960 or 1961. *Garrett Freightlines*

Survival in the trucking industry has required meeting tough challenges from its earliest days. Pioneer drivers and owners faced riding on rough city streets on solid rubber tires; driving in open cabs in the cold winters; driving trucks only barely powerful enough to pull those long, steep grades; unloading your own truck before the days of dock workers; or doing your own mechanical repairs out on the road before the days of service calls. In those early years of trucking, drivers often started their own one-truck companies. Among them were men like Clarence Garrett, Thomas Carter, Owen Orr, Carroll and Galen Rouch, Ben Spector, Mose Wilson, A. B. Crichton, Sr., Ray Smith, Richard Riss, J. W. Ringsby, Steve Kramer, and Michael Murphy, to mention a few.

The routine for ordering or buying a truck at that time is the same as today. Buyers decided what and how much they wanted to haul and ordered accordingly. The variety of body types included tank bodies for hauling gasoline and other liquids; flatbeds for hauling lumber; a screen-side body with side curtains and canvas roof for hauling fruit and produce; and dump bodies for hauling coal, sand, or gravel; among other types. Farmers, furniture makers, appliance manufacturers, construction companies, grain mills, lumber companies, gas companies, paper mills, fruit and produce dealers, steel mills, and baggage companies joined commercial freight haulers to make up the burgeoning truck market. The cost of purchasing a truck depended on the size, the weight rating, and the model classification and options according to what the customer wanted.

As we strive for the future, it remains to be seen which trucks will be there. The future in the trucking industry will be very challenging. We must remember the people and things that paved the way for our trucking industry today and in its future.

CHAPTER ONE

THE INTERNAL COMBUSTION AGE BEGINS

Before the days of the motor trucks, horses and wagons were the most common means of transporting freight. Most teams were made up of two to four horses, along with one or two drivers. As we have double and triple trailers today, early freight haulers also used two and three wagons, depending on the cargo. There were wagons that were made for different types of hauling. The same types of commodities that we haul today were also hauled in the days of horses and wagons.

The motor truck made its appearance around 1900. The first ones were somewhat small, but over the course of the first few years of the new century, they started to increase in size. Every year, more new truck manufacturers came on the scene-it's estimated that there were at this time about 1,800 different brand names of trucks. Some of them existed for only one year, and some others maybe two or three. However, some of these pioneer truck makers still exist today, such as Kenworth, Freightliner, Peterbilt, Mack, White, International, Sterling, and Chevrolet.

Many of the early trucks had to take a beating because the roads and streets in those days were either dirt or cobblestone, which made for a very uncomfortable ride. As they traveled these rough roads and streets, it put them to the test to see how much of a beating they could withstand. Common problems included the drive chain coming off the sprocket, chunks of rubber breaking off the wheels, as well as broken wheels and axles caused by the treacherous roads.

Trucking companies were starting to form, although they were small compared to the truck fleets of today. There were many different models offered with many different types of bodies available for the different types of hauling.

Most early trucks did not have much to offer in the way of comfort. Some had an open cab and if you were lucky, you could get side curtains. Comfort features were considered options by a lot of the manufacturers.

During the 1910s, traveling from New York City to Philadelphia would have been a long-distance run. There were many trucking companies, but most were small, consisting of two, three, four, or five trucks. Some manufacturers hauled their own merchandise from city to city by using their own fleet. Demand continued to grow, and more trucking companies came into being. Among those that existed in 1917 were the Davis & Durham Express of Philadelphia; Krueger Cartage; Hayes Transfer & Storage Co.; Adams Express Co.; Yates Bros. Transfer & Storage in Joliet, Illinois; Wells Fargo & Express Co.; Harvey's Local Express; Geo. Smith General Hauling of Stratman, Missouri; Mahefky & Sons General Hauling in Hazelwood, Pennsylvania; Sharp's Express; and Adams Transfer & Storage Co.

The first 20 years were not easy in the new-born trucking industry. Competition among the companies was great, and it ended up to be a battle for survival of the fittest. In 1917, there were 372 companies that manufactured trucks. Just prior to the 1920s, there were a total of over 419,000 motor trucks in the United States, with the mid-Atlantic states having over 122,000 of them. The new-born trucking industry was to make them or break them.

Although trucks went into the war, they not only served their purpose, but at the same time, it was also an experimenting period. I'm sure they had problems out in the war areas, but from those problems, the manufacturers then knew what change had to be made to better their product.

This scene is in Public Square in Montgomery, Alabama, where farmers came to sell their baled cotton. Horses and wagons were still the means for hauling the crop to market.

This Mercury truck was probably number one in the fleet of the F. Landon Cartage Co. of Chicago, Illinois, established in 1892. Mercury trucks were made in Chicago from 1911 to 1917. *F. Landon Cartage Co.*

Banfield Moving & Storage Co. of New Jersey got its start with Chase trucks in the 1910s. Banfield later on became anagent for North American Van Lines of Ft. Wayne, Indiana. Chase trucks were made in Syracuse, New York, from 1907 to 1918. *Harry Patterson*

Van Brunt & Sons, Inc. of Matawan, New Jersey, got its start in 1889 when William Van Brunt purchased the steamboat company. Coaches and wagons were used for 23 years until the company made the switch from wagons to motor trucks. This 1912 Federal was truck No. 2 in the fleet, a rather large truck for the time. The load consists of wooden crates and barrels. Federal trucks were made from 1914 to 1959. *Van Brunt & Sons, Inc.*

The following chart is information taken from Motor Trucks of America, published by the B.F. Goodrich Co. in 1917.

Make	Model	Capacity	Horsepower	Price
Atterbury	7E	5 tons	42	$4,275.00
Beech Creek	B	3 tons	32.6	3,850.00
Modern	30	1 ton	27	1,500.00
Corbett	B	2-1/2 tons	40	2,650.00
FWD	B	3 tons	45	4,000.00
Schacht	1-1/2 ton	1-1/2 tons	40	2,650.00
Hahn	E	2 tons	40	2,250.00
Lange	B	2-1/2 tons	35	2,550.00
Maccar	U	5-1/2 tons	40	4,500.00
Pierce Arrow	5 ton	5 tons	42	4,500.00
Rowe	CDW	2 tons	52	2,800.00
Standard	65	3-1/2 tons	55	2,850.00
Sterling	7 ton	7 tons	52	5,250.00
Velie	25	2 tons		2,250.00
Wichita	Q	5 tons	40	3,850.00

Back in the mid-1910s, many new trucking companies were getting into the hauling business, including the Long Island Rural Motor Express Co., located in New York City. Truck No. 24 was a Day-Elder 5-ton job. The body was 16 feet long and 8 feet high. The cab and the body both had weather curtains. Day-Elder trucks were made from 1918 to 1931 in Newark, New Jersey. *Ron Adams collection*

National Transportation Co. was from Bridgeport, Connecticut. Truck No. 9 was a Ward La France made in Elmira, New York. Almost all the trucks in those days had solid rubber tires. Note the fine pinstriping on the frame, cab, and wheels. *National Transportation Co.*

Midwest was one of the many trucking companies with headquarters in Chicago. In the 1950s, Midwest Co. merged with Emery Transportation Co. to become Midwest Emery Freight System. The truck is believed to be a GMC or an Autocar. *Midwest Emery Freight System*

CHAPTER TWO
ROADS TO SUCCESS IN THE 1920s

Trucks changed rapidly during the postwar 1920s. Solid rubber tires faded out as balloon tires entered the picture, and closed cabs replaced open cabs as a standard feature. Bigger trucks could haul more freight. More and better roads were built to accommodate the larger vehicles. With imprived roads and more powerful trucks, freight could be hauled longer distances.

By 1920, trailers were built to create the now well-known combination tractor-trailer. Trailers were still relatively short—12 to 18 feet. Trailer makers included some names we still recognize today: Fruehauf, Hobbs, Trailmobile, Kingham, Mack, Utility, Reliance, Wilson, Highway, Williamsen, Keystone, Nabors, Hyde, Watson, Dominion,

Edwards, Byron, Ohio, Warner, King, and Lapeer. The bodies that were available were about the same type as for the straight trucks. The prices of the trailers ranged from $500 to $3,500.

In addition to the tractor-trailer combination, the truck-trailer also appeared on the nation's roadways for the first time. More-powerful engines allowed a straight truck to pull a four-wheel trailer as well. Double trailers were also being used at this time. Although truck-trailer combinations were not popular in the East, the idea caught on in the wide-open West, and is still common there today. Through the 1920s, the number of truck manufacturers decreased while the number of trucking companies increased.

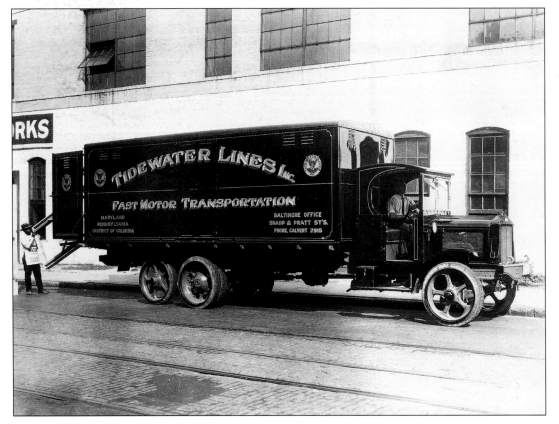

Tidewater Lines probably became known as Tidewater Express Lines of Baltimore, Maryland, in its later years. This model 52 White had a third axle and chain drive and was probably the first truck in the fleet—a sharp-looking outfit for its time. *White Motor Co.*

By the end of the 1920s, longer runs were starting to be made, which meant more options had to be offered by the manufacturer for hauling more freight and driver options. Trailers got longer to haul more freight, and sleeper cabs-known as an integral sleepers-came into being. All truck manufacturers of the times offered sleeper cabs on both the straight truck and tractors.

The booming economic times of the 1920s helped establish the trucking industry as a viable long-distance hauling method. As the automobile became more common, drivers wanted better roads. More improved roads opened up the country for truckers to haul nearly any kind of cargo to ever more far-reaching corners of the land.

Leonard Bros. Storage Co. of Detroit, Michigan, was a local and long-distance moving and warehouse company. Truck No. 9 was an Autocar. Truck-trailer combinations like this one were somewhat common at the time. Solid rubber tires were still standard. *Ron Adams collection*

Although the license plate on the tractor shows 1941, the truck is an early-1920s AC Mack. The Cleveland Cartage Company of Cleveland, Ohio, was the proud owner of this Mack workhorse, which was still using solid rubber tires. The make of the low-bed trailer is unknown, but it was built tough for the job and also has solid rubber tires. Note the White in the background. *Cleveland Cartage Co.*

In the early 1920s, there were many moving companies in business with many more to follow. Neptune Moving Co. of New Rochelle, New York, was ready to move with this 1923 AB Mack. The colors of this truck are believed to be light yellow with red lettering—Neptune's known colors in later years. *Ron Adams collection*

Beginning early on, there were many different types of truck bodies. This is a rack-side body on a 1928 Studebaker that hauled many different kinds of commodities. Owner Manning Patrick hauled out of New Brunswick, New Jersey. *Ron Adams collection*

What this huge pipe will be used for is anybody's guess, but we do know that it's being hauled by a 1929 model 5IT White. Although this truck, No. 18, shows some use by the dented fenders, owner C. E. Musselwhite of Houston, Texas, was proud of it for getting the job done. *White Motor Co.*

Sometimes the load on a truck gets more attention than the truck does. This load speaks for itself. The late-1920s AB Mack, owned by Desert Express, has a full load of Al Capone's cough syrup. *Desert Express*

Banfield Moving & Storage Co. of Atlantic Highlands, New Jersey, was proud of this late-1920s Diamond T. By the number on the truck, it looks like Banfield had a sizable fleet by this time. As agent for North American Van Lines, Banfield's motto was "Not the oldest—just the best." *Harry Patterson*

This 1929 Seldon RoadMaster was owned by the Fisher-Gilder Co., which was an agent for the Mayflower Transit Co. in Youngstown, Ohio. The Mayflower graphics, with the yellow and green colors, were the same for many years. *Ron Adams collection*

Truck No. 14 is a late-1920s Schacht in service for "Al" Naish Moving & Storage Co. of Cincinnati, Ohio, another agent for the Mayflower Transit Co. *Ron Adams collection*

Trucks for the moving companies all seemed to have the same basic body style like this late 1920s Gramm, made in Lima, Ohio. Truck No. 20 was owned by Joplin Transfer & Storage Co. of Joplin, Missouri. Note the simple three-digit phone number. The tires are General cords. *Ron Adams collection*

Although the make of the truck could be a Moreland, the truck body and trailer are both by Utility. Crated merchandise and bagged feed was the load for the day. The driver is wearing his unloading chaps and shin guards for protection from injury. The company is also unknown. *Utility Trailer Co.*

CHAPTER THREE

SURVIVING & THRIVING IN THE 1930s

While the stock market crash of October 29, 1929, and the subsequent Depression was devastating for many Americans, those desperate times did ultimately create opportunities for some. With consumers unable to buy, manufacturers were unable to sell, and the need for hauling no-longer-affordable goods to market diminished substantially. Numerous trucking companies had to call it quits.

But for others, hard work, perseverance, and more than a little luck paid off. In the first part of the decade, they focused on survival, and if they could make money at it, they hauled it. The trucking industry got a boost in 1933 with the repeal of Prohibition, which opened the tap for legal beer and alcohol sales, spawning a new generation of haulers to meet the need.

Among the survivors of this decade of desperation were Owen Orr, who founded Motor Cargo, Inc.; Leland James of Consolidated Freightways; Carroll and Galen Rouch of Roadway Express; W. S. Hatch & Co.; Earl Condon of Old Dominion Freight Lines; the Beam Brothers of Carolina Freight Carriers; Arno Dalby of Time Freight, Inc.; James Ryder of Ryder Truck Lines; Tom Carter of Interstate Motor Lines; and E. Ward King of Mason and Dixon Lines.

Coming into the decade, companies were small. But as the Depression waned, truck owners starting investing in

No job was too big or too small for Bigge Drayage Co. of Oakland, California, in the early 1930s. Moving the coastal artillery gun shown here required some special equipment. This model DC Sterling was the power source to pull a load this big, although it looks like it was getting a helping hand from another vehicle attached by two cables to the tractor. The guns were deployed along the Atlantic and Pacific coasts as a defense against enemy ships. *Ron Adams collection*

better and more modern equipment. And company owner Leland James even started to manufacture his own trucks. Bigger trucks and trailers and better engineering allowed trucking companies to haul more freight per run. Refrigeration became more common during the decade, with ancestors of the now-ubiquitous reefers, or refrigerated trucks or trailers, hitting the highways to haul perishables.

The Motor Carrier Act of 1935 regulated what the companies could charge to haul freight, known as rates, the number of hours that drivers were allowed to drive, the area a company could operate in, what the companies could haul, and where.

Driving trucks back in the 1930s was not easy. Although the highways were improving, riding comfort was not what it is today. Most of the roads were two-lane highways and in the mountainous regions, a driver could wear himself out by all the frequent shifting. *The First 50 Years*, a history of Consolidated Freightways, recounts a run by a C.F. driver in 1937 from San Francisco to Reno on old Route 40. From Roseville, California, to Reno, a distance of 125 miles, the driver shifted gears 844 times. On a 36-mile stretch from Roseville to Colfax, he shifted 318 times in 1 hour and 58 minutes. And on another stretch from Fox Farm to Donner Summit, a distance of 3.2 miles, the driver shifted 59 times in 18 minutes. A lot of trucks at this time had two sticks to shift, compared to one stick or an automatic today.

Drivers also encountered problems such as flat tires, mechanical trouble, and-like today-those bad winter snowstorms that could cause delays for days. There was no airconditioning, no power steering, no air-ride seats, no walk-in sleepers, no CB radios, and big truck stops were unheard of. Roadside diners and gas stations, some of which had bunk houses, were stopping places for truck drivers. The conditions were not the best, but it was all part of the job.

Drivers in those days earned their money. The pay for one company, for example, was $.75 per hour for a 12-hour day at 250 days per year. Drivers were allowed to drive anywhere from 8 to 12 consecutive hours per day. Although the work day was tough, many drivers enjoyed their jobs. The organizing of the unions is something that the trucking companies did not want, but it became a reality. For the drivers, it was a good thing, but in some ways, it was a bad thing for the companies. A good example of this was in the mid 1970s when a three-year strike against Ringsby Truck Lines of Denver, Colorado, closed the company down for good.

As roads improved in the 1930s, trips could be made faster. A run from Pittsburgh to New York City took about 12 to 14 hours, which was good at the time. In 1932, a 1,116-mile round trip from San Francisco to Salt Lake City with two drivers was made in 33 hours for Intermountain Motor Freight. Another western run for Los Angeles-New Mexico and Texas Motor Express took 36 hours from Los Angeles to El Paso with a tractor-trailer. In 1936, Mason & Dixon Lines made a run from Atlanta to New York City, a total of 942 miles, in 40 hours.

In the mid-1930s, the design and dimensions of trucks and trailers began to change. In 1931, trailer length varied from 14 to 20 feet. By the mid- to late 1930s, the length

This 1931 model 64 White looks like it was probably the truck that got business going for Zeno Bros. Trucking in Akron, Ohio. The tractor has a five-man cab and cab lights and a set of air horns on the right fender. *Ron Adams collection*

Riss and Co. of Denver, Colorado, was a refrigerated hauler from its beginning. In 1932, Riss later moved its office to Kansas City, Missouri, and also hauled dry freight and had a steel division. Riss still had its reefer division into the 1970s. The trucks are "A" model Internationals. According to the number on the cab door of the left-hand truck, Riss must have had at least 18 tractor-trailer units at this time. *Highway Trailer Co.*

increased to 28 and 32 feet. Rounded fronts began to show up on trailers. Body builders Fruehauf and Heil, among others, created streamlined trailers and bodies. Trucks and tractors started featuring rounded fenders, pointed grills, and slanted windshields as the streamlining craze overtook industrial design. White, for example, hired industrial designer

Count Sakhnoffsky to create the desired look.

As the decade ended, trucking companies and private company fleets were on the increase. Some of this was due to the war in Europe. The United States started selling materials to the European countries for war use, and the fastest way to get the goods from factory to ships was by truck.

Harley L. Babel Truck Service of Sterling, Illinois, was the proud owner of this early-1930s Hendrickson tractor and Highway combination freight and livestock trailer. Notice the triangle window on the cab behind the windshield. Dual air horns give it a customized look. *Highway Trailer Co.*

Double trailers were among the different combinations in the 1930s. This outfit belonged to Universal Carloading and Distribution Co. The Stewart sleeper cab tractor pulled the two Highway trailers. Note the three-piece windshield. The truck is running on Firestone tires. *Highway Trailer Co.*

In the early 1930s, sleeper cabs started to become more popular for overnight runs. Truck No. 15 was a DC model Sterling for Bates Motor Transport Lines that served Illinois, Indiana, Michigan, and Kentucky. Trailer No. 15 is a Highway insulated with aircraft insulation. Note the lights on the trailer, which was unusual for that time. *Highway Trailer Co.*

The following list shows 20 trucking companies that were still in existence in 1940, and the size of their fleets:

	Company of trucks	Number of tractors	Number of trailers	Number vehicles	Total
1	Alabama Highway Express	14	78	82	174
2	Geo. F. Alger Co.	28	115	238	381
3	Baltimore Transfer Co.	33	72	110	215
4	Brady Transfer & Storage Co.	35	115	155	305
5	Commercial Motor Freight	140	159	280	579
6	Consolidated Motor Lines	92	275	345	712
7	Galveston Truck Lines	0	28	28	56
8	Gay's Express, Inc.	85	38	45	168
9	Globe Cartage Co.	0	107	107	214
10	Horlacher Delivery Service	142	28	46	216
11	Horton Motor Lines	121	300	300	721
12	Huber & Huber Motor Express	130	65	74	269
13	Interstate Dispatch, Inc.	182	72	110	364
14	Keeshin Freight Lines	233	460	911	1,604
15	Long Transportation Co.	38	78	88	204
16	Midnite Express, Inc.	40	50	50	147
17	Roadway Express, Inc.	114	194	197	505
18	Robinson Transportation Co.	0	6	11	11
19	Rogers Motor Lines	11	9	11	31
20	St. Johnsbuy Trucking Co.	60	60	38	8

Maccar Trucks were made from 1914 to 1931 in Scranton, Pennsylvania. This 1931 Model was owned by M. Moran Transportation Lines, serving northern New York state. In the early 1930s, almost any kind of truck and trailer combination could be seen, such as this truck and double trailer combo. *Ron Adams collection*

Crown Motor Freight of Paterson, New Jersey, covered the three-state area of New York, New Jersey, and Pennsylvania. This BM Mack with integral sleeper and Van Den Berg trailer hauled the freight in the tri-state area. *Ron Adams collection*

Photographed in 1938, these BM Mack sleeper cab tractors—which got the job done very well—and Fruehauf trailers await their turn to leave on their next run. Shirks Motor Express of Lancaster, Pennsylvania, was the proud owner of these trucks. *John Hiestand*

Integral sleepers were popular across the country. This early-1930s model FC Sterling was owned by Arrowhead Freightlines of Los Angeles, California. The long wheelbase and sleeper cab give this truck a tough look, and the lettering makes for a rather striking appearance. Arrowhead became part of the Asbury Transportation Co. and in 1956 was purchased by Interstate Motor Lines in Salt Lake City, Utah. *Ernest Sternberg*

This LaFrance-Republic, a straight truck without a sleeper cab, was owned by Boston Trucking Co. of Boston. Note the cab's single marker light. *Ron Adams collection*

Trucks such as this one were a common sight in the western states. This six-wheel Fageol truck-trailer combination was capable of hauling a 39,000-pound payload. Consolidated Freight Lines of Portland, Oregon, was the proud owner. *Consolidated Freightways*

Wooster Express, Inc. of Hartford, Connecticut, was proud of this mid-1930s BX Mack. Trucks like this were common on the East Coast as tractor-trailers started appearing more and more. Note the pinstriping to fancy up the truck. *Mack Trucks*

Thompson Trucking Co. of Cliffside, New Jersey, was a long-distance carrier. Truck No. 18 is a Hahn that was made in Hamburg, Pennsylvania. Note the seven identical row houses in the background. *Hahn Motors*

This mid-1930s Sterling was seen traveling the California highways for Pacific Freight Lines. Many trucks of the 1930s were still chain-driven. The body and the trailer were made by the Weber Body and Trailer Co. *Ernest Stennberg*

Back in the early 1930s, Kenworth was making big trucks like this one. Associated Truck Lines of Portland, Oregon, was the owner of No. 3, known as Betty "D." The "Ship by Truck" emblem was already around in those years. Note the headlights on this truck—the special narrow-prism lens lamps were called "Woodlites" and were usually found on luxury cars of the time, such as Cadillacs, Auburns, and Lincolns. *Kenworth Truck Co.*

In its early years, Hahn Motors in Hamburg, Pennsylvania, made not only fire trucks, but also commercial trucks. Eckert's Transfer was a Hahn customer with this typical household goods truck of the time. *Hahn Motors*

This 1934 CH Mack, tractor No. 4, looks like one of the first trucks for Werner Transportation Co. of Minneapolis, Minnesota. The colors of this rig are probably red and gray, since those were the Werner colors in later years. The extras on this truck include air horns, spotlight, and road sanders, which, along with all the chrome, make for a sharp-looking tractor. *Mack Trucks*

Sleeper cab tractors such as this BM Mack in 1934 were very popular with a lot of trucking companies. Glendenning of St. Paul, Minnesota, was one of the many companies that used sleeper cab tractors to run between St. Paul and Chicago. *Mack Trucks*

In many cases it is hard to tell what a truck has loaded as it goes down the highway with its closed body. Judging from the sticker on the body, it looks like White Line Transfer and Storage Co. of Des Moines, Iowa, is hauling liquor with this 1934 BM Mack. The body was made by Lagerquist Auto Body Co. in Des Moines. *Mack Trucks*

Another truck from the later 1930s for Consolidated Freight Lines of Portland, Oregon, is this 1937 Kenworth. At this time, Consolidated covered the Pacific Northwest and into the Rocky Mountain states. The name was later changed to Consolidated Freightways. This style of Kenworth was known as the "shovel nose" because of the look of its grille. *Kenworth Truck Co.*

Four-to-one was the way to haul cars in the 1930s. New York Car Carriers, Inc. of Buffalo, New York, used this 1936 30MT Mack Jr. to haul this load of brand-new Plymouth cars and one panel truck. Note that there is very little space between the bottom of the trailer and the top of the rear axle tires on the tractor. Lee tires are used on the trailer. *Mack Trucks*

This streamlined 1938 EC Mack was one of 123 made from 1936 to 1941. Boulevard Moving and Warehouse Co. of Milwaukee, Wisconsin, was an agent for Aero Mayflower Transit Co. Given the history of Mayflower color schemes, this truck was likely painted black, green, and yellow. *Mack Trucks*

Interstate Motor Lines of Salt Lake City, Utah, served five western states around 1938. This "J" series Sterling was one of a variety of different makes and types of equipment that Interstate used in its fleet throughout its operations. *Ernest Sternberg*

Hanna Transfer Co. of Oil City, Pennsylvania, agent for North American Van Lines in 1938, used this unknown make on a Ford chassis. Given the color scheme for North American Van Lines in the 1950s and 1960s, the truck colors were probably maroon, cream, and black. *Ron Adams collection*

Driving in every kind of condition is all part of a truck driver's job. This driver had to navigate this 1938 700 Series White & Fruehauf Aero-Van trailer for Miami Transportation Co. of Cincinnati, Ohio, through several inches of snow. Chains were added for traction. *Miami Transportation Co.*

Western Trucking Co. of St. Louis, Missouri, had this circa 1939 Hendrickson, owned by Joe Mohl, running in its fleet. The Keystone trailer, hooked to the Hendrickson, makes a good-looking rig. Notice the Lincoln Greyhound ornament on the hood. *Western Trucking Co.*

Back in the 1930s, Roadway Express was a big carrier, covering almost all of the eastern United States. This picture was taken in 1939 at Roadway's Dallas, Texas, terminal. The 1938 "D" model International was owned by Buck Hartline of Akron, Ohio. *S. L. Hartline*

White WA models were popular with many trucking companies. Mason & Dixon Lines of Kingsport, Tennessee, was a big White user in the 1930s and into the 1960s. Trucks like this one could be seen running up the East Coast into New York City. *Mason & Dixon Lines*

This was the first truck that Consolidated Freightways built in its Salt Lake City shop. It was the design of Leland James. The first few trucks were named Freightways, but were later named Freightliner. James wanted trucks designed and built a certain way, but no manufacturer would do what he wanted, so the company designed and built its own trucks. *Freightliner Corp.*

CHAPTER FOUR
HAULING FOR FREEDOM IN THE 1940s

With the bombing of Pearl Harbor on December 7, 1941, the United States was dragged into World War II. Most domestic manufacturers, including truck builders, turned their attention to the production of war supplies. At the same time, rationing of raw materials and gasoline held back the development of commercial trucking on the home front-unless it was connected to the war effort. Only 1 out of every 10 vehicles manufactured went for commercial use. Trucking companies were called upon to do more with less-in addition to normal hauling duties, they hauled incredible amounts of war material. Being unable to acquire new trucks, companies were forced to keep many older trucks running longer, past their prime, to get the job done!

During the war, certain truck manufacturing companies made certain types of military vehicles. Diamond T, Ward LaFrance, and Kenworth made wreckers. Autocar, International, and White made half-tracks. Mack and White made

trucks to do the big moving, such as construction equipment and army tanks. Diamond T was also a prime builder for moving tanks.

Overseas sales of trucks dropped sharply. The reason was because after the war, any military trucks that were left behind were sold to other countries and were modified for hauling needs until the European manufacturers could get their plants back in operation after having them destroyed during the war.

Some trucking companies did have government contracts to haul war materials. Some trucking companies, especially auto haulers, even converted some of their trailers to be used to haul airplanes.

Once the war ended in 1945, the production of vehicles returned to normal. Immediately following the war, however, there was somewhat of a shortage of trucks. Some fleet owners and independent drivers bought excess military

Designing new and better ways to haul was a priority in the trucking industry. Auto haulers were often at the forefront of development, with new configurations that could carry cars more efficiently. This 1940 Chevrolet owned by ARCO Auto Carriers of Chicago, is hauling four new Nash cars. *A. E. Woodworth Photography*

North Alabama Motor Express covered a route between Birmingham, Alabama, and Columbus, Georgia. Truck No. 55 is a 1940 EG Mack. "Tommy" appears to be the driver's name. *Mack Trucks*

trucks-they may not have been exactly the trucks they wanted, but the hauling business was there and this was the only way to survive until the manufacturers could fill the demand.

In many cases, manufacturers' initial postwar models were duplicates of the final prewar trucks. Completely new postwar models included the International W series cab targeted for use in the West, offered in both conventional and cab-over-engine styles in 1946. Mack also came out with its famous LT model for heavy western operators. Some truck manufacturers, such as Mack and International, had their own engines but most relied on established engine makers such as Buda, Cummins, and Waukesha (diesel) and Continental and Hall-Scott (gas). In the late 1940s, some new models by GMC and White, with the 3000 low cabover engine (COE), hit the highways, while in 1950 Autocar came out with its new driver cab.

The allowable length of trailers increased to 35 feet. Lighter aluminum trailers were becoming more popular. Trucking companies were building up new fleets of equipment to replace the worn-out equipment that was used so hard during the war. The Highway Transport Department called for the construction of 1,063,000 trucks, 50,000 trailers, and 250,000 bodies for trucks for 1946.

It was also a time of consolidation, as some companies expanded their operations by taking over other operations. Probably the biggest such acquisition was in 1946, when Denver Chicago Trucking Co. bought out the operations of the Adams Transfer and Storage Co. of Kansas City, Missouri, making Denver Chicago the first coast-to-coast carrier.

For cross-country hauling, most carriers relied on interlining. Not unlike the railroad system, interlining allowed a trucking company to send a load bound for a city outside of its operating territory by hooking the trailer to the tractor of another trucking company that had authority to haul to the destination city. For example, Pacific Intermountain Express (P-I-E) in Oakland, California, covered the western states and inland through Kansas, Nebraska, Iowa, Missouri, and Illinois. P-I-E had terminals throughout its operating territory, with Chicago being its easternmost terminal. If P-I-E picked up a trailer load in Portland, Oregon, that was bound for Jersey City, New Jersey, that trailer would be routed through the P-I-E relay system into its terminal. Once the trailer reached Chicago, it was taken to the terminal of another trucking company that had the authority to take it to Jersey City.

As trucking companies and truck manufacturers caught up following the war, they paved the way for a booming decade to come in the 1950s.

J. E. Thompson, the owner and operator of this 1940 UGOT Autocar tractor and Trailmobile trailer, was proud of his rig. Thompson was leased out to LeCrone Motor Transport Lines of Columbus, Ohio, and had a connection with Benedict Lines, Inc. This is a rather neat-looking combination. *Autocar Trucks*

Modern Transfer Co. of Allentown, Pennsylvania, served New York, New Jersey, Pennsylvania, Maryland, Delaware, and the District of Columbia. Modern was an all-Mack fleet, and this 1940 EHT was one of the fleet with a Fruehauf trailer. *Mack Trucks*

H & NT (Houston and North Texas Motor Freight Lines) operated out of Dallas, Texas. This is a WA18T White tractor with a Fruehauf trailer in 1941, both apparently painted silver. *White Motor Co.*

This WA18T early-1940s White tractor and Fruehauf trailer are also from the Texas area. Red Arrow Freight Lines of Houston survived through the years up until the 1980s. This tractor had a larger engine that was nicknamed "Super-Power." *White Motor Co.*

Georgia to Illinois seemed to be a popular area to run for a number of southern trucking companies, including Georgia Highway Express, Inc. of Atlanta, using this White tractor and Fruehauf trailer. *Ron Adams collection*

In the early 1940s, travelers along the California highways could see this Autocar tractor pulling a set of double tanker trailers for Lamb Transportation. *Autocar Trucks*

Garrett Freight Lines of Pocatello, Idaho, was one of many companies that ran these truck-trailer combinations in the western states. These green and yellow rigs could be seen in almost all of the 11 western states. In this case, a Kenworth truck was the source of power on this run. *Garrett Freightlines*

This early-1940s brute is an "R" Model Sterling. The tank body, which can haul 3,450 gallons as well as pull the trailer carrying another 3,600 gallons of gas, is manufactured by Peerless Trailer and Body Co. AB Transportation is the owner of the truck-trailer rig. *Photo Art Commercial Studios*

Freightliner made cab-over-engine trucks, but they also made some conventional trucks like this 1942 model. Consolidated Freightways was the only company using Freightliner trucks, since Consolidated owned the Freightliner Corp. *Freightliner Corp.*

30187, C60T-161½ Spec.
3-17-41

Some trucking companies were contracted to specific shippers. Carter Bros., Inc., of Richmond, Virginia, was contracted to A & P Co. One of the trucks in its fleet was a 1941 C60T Autocar sleeper that pulled a 24-foot Fruehauf trailer. *Autocar Trucks*

During the 1940s, Branch Motor Express, Inc. of Brooklyn, New York, served New York, New Jersey, Pennsylvania, and Maryland with this "K" Model International tractor. *Branch Motor Express*

This tandem-axle, long-wheelbase "K" Model International sleeper was somewhat rare. These were mainly used in the Midwest. American Transit Lines of Chicago used this one to pull a grain trailer, though it probably contained steel. *Joe Wanchura*

Roadway Express of Akron, Ohio, used this "K" Model International during World War II. Roadway was one of the larger trucking companies during the war, displaying the American eagle to buy war bonds on the Fruehauf trailer. Detroit, Charlotte, and Akron were only a few of the many terminals Roadway had at this time. *Roadway Express*

Tough trucks were made for big heavy loads. This wartime Federal was the truck elected to do this job. It was one of many types and makes of trucks produced for the military, then sold to private carriers as surplus after the war. William Higgins and Sons, Inc. Trucking and Rigging, of Buffalo, New York, took on the job and had the ingredients to get it done right, with the Federal tractor and unknown make of low-bed trailer.

L. R. Elliott Trucking, Inc. of San Diego, California, offered refrigerated service. This 1941, DC 10062 Autocar with a 173-inch wheelbase pulled the Fruehauf 35-foot trailer. *Autocar Trucks*

This DC 10062 with a 157-inch wheelbase and a Fruehauf trailer is owned by System Freight Service of Los Angeles, California. The company served eight states along the Pacific Coast and Southwest. *Autocar Trucks*

Southern California seemed to be a hot spot for Autocar trucks. This is a single-axle DC 100 Autocar pulling double milk tanker trailers for Lamb Transportation Co. of Long Beach, California. Looking at the numbers of the tractor (70), and trailers (88), it seems like Lamb had a sizable fleet in 1941. *Autocar Trucks*

Another Autocar from southern California is this DC 10062 on a 162-inch wheelbase pulling a Utility six-wheel, or tri-axle, trailer. La Salle Trucking Co. of San Diego was probably a contract hauler for Aztec Brewing Co. of the same city. It's anybody's guess what the color scheme could be, along with the eye-catching graphics. *Autocar Trucks*

This 1941 photo came from McLean Trucking Co., Inc. of Winston-Salem, North Carolina. The Mack tractor looks like it could be a late 1930s version, since the EH was made from 1936 to 1950. The style of the trailer looks like it could be a Fruehauf. It's a rather neat-looking combination. *McLean Trucking Co.*

Unit No. 8 is a circa World War II Peterbilt truck-trailer livestock rig. The early models had four circular holes in the bumper. The rectangular Peterbilt emblem was used up until 1951 or 1952. Batteate Livestock Transportation proudly owned this outfit. *Peterbilt Motor Co.*

Highway Express Lines of Philadelphia, Pennsylvania, was a relatively small company, given the area it covered: eastern Pennsylvania, New Jersey, New York, Maryland, and Virginia. This mid-1940s Ford flatbed trailer was probably used to haul baled or rolled textiles. *Ed Brinker Photography*

This 1946 Autocar model C70T on a 148-inch wheelbase and Trailmobile trailer was owned by Del Parker of Allentown, Pennsylvania. Del leased his truck to various companies and later drove for Associated Transport Co. of New York City. *Autocar Trucks*

Highway Express also used this mid-1940s "C" Model Autocar tractor and reefer trailer with a Thermo-King refrigeration unit. *Ed Brinker Photography*

While most manufacturers made trucks for general hauling, a few were specialized. FWD specialized in four-wheel-drive trucks, thus the letters FWD. The company did make some trucks for general use into the 1970s. This photo is dated June 10, 1946, so we can assume that this is a World War II truck. The trailer brand is unknown, but its husky-built is a brother to the husky-built see above FWD. Les. Johnson Cartage Co. of Denmark, Wisconsin, is moving what appears to be a piece of highway construction machinery. *Les Johnson Cartage Co.*

One of the many trucking companies of the 1940s was Safeway Truck Lines of Chicago. The circa mid-1940s WA model White sleeper and Fruehauf trailer is unit No. 60. Safeway was a dry freight and reefer hauler, and in the 1960s, it became part of the Midwest Emery Freight System, also of Chicago. *Joe Wanchura*

Inland Motor Freight, Inc. of Spokane, Washington, was a Pacific Northwest Carrier that operated in Washington, Oregon, and Idaho. This mid-1940s Peterbilt truck-trailer combination was typical of the equipment many companies used in this area at this time. *Joe Wanchura*

Aero Mayflower Transit Co. of Indianapolis, Indiana, was a nationwide household goods carrier. This WA model White sleeper and Fruehauf moving trailer make a very attractive combination. Imagine this in color with the Mayflower colors of red, green, and yellow. *Jones Photography*

Allied Van Lines of Broadview, Illinois, was another nationwide household goods carrier. Dunn Bros. Storage and Warehouse, Inc. of Chicago is an agent for Allied. This WA122 White and Fruehauf moving trailer is painted in the orange-and-black Allied colors. *White Motor Co.*

Berea, Ohio, was the home office for Mack Bros. Moving and Trucking, Inc. (no connection to Mack Trucks). Mack Bros. used this mid-1940s Diamond T and Fruehauf trailer to move freight. It's not the biggest tractor that Diamond T offered, but the big saddle tanks and sanders give it the big look. *Smith Bros. Photography–Detroit*

Another company from the Pacific Northwest was Bestway Motor Freight of Seattle. A lot of the companies from this area were smaller but they served their customers well. Many of these companies did, however, use big equipment such as this circa 1946 Sterling and 1950s Brown trailer. *Joe Wanchura*

Peoria Cartage Co. of Peoria, Illinois, was a medium-size regional company. A KB8 International and Fruehauf half-closed and half-open top trailer were used in the over-the-road fleet, circa 1947. *Ron Adams collection*

Daigh & Stewart Truck Co. was a heavy hauling company out of Bakersfield, California. A DC100 Autocar hauls this load of structural steel. *Ron Adams collection*

Back in the 1940s, it seemed like a lot of truckers had their own ways of engineering different types of rigs. Elmer Hicks of Martin, South Dakota, came up with his own version of a truck-trailer combination. This "K" model International had a short Trailmobile tank on the chassis with a Trailmobile pull-trailer. *Mile High Photography*

Consolidated Freightways of Portland, Oregon, manufactured its own trucks starting in 1937 with the Freightliner. This Freightliner chassis, body, and trailer were built in the Portland factory around 1947. Consolidated ran a lot of these truck-trailer combinations wherever possible. After the war, Freightliner began to sell trucks to other carriers. *Photo Art Commercial Studios*

Los Angeles-Seattle Motor Express, Inc. (LASME) of Seattle hauled dry freight and refrigerated products along the Pacific Coast. Its equipment was basically the same type that other western carriers used, like this circa 1947 Peterbilt with Brown body and pull-trailer. LASME in its later years merged with Denver Chicago Trucking Co. and Time Freight, Inc. to form the giant carrier Time-DC. *Los Angeles-Seattle Motor Express, Inc.*

Another truck-trailer combination was this livestock hauler owned by Vernon Livestock Trucking Co. The name on the running board, A. F. Cummins, is probably the driver. Note the stack location on this circa 1947 Peterbilt. *Courtesy Stan Holtzman*

A lot of trucks in the 1940s were built "truck tough," as seen in this photo. Based on the pictures taken by Joe Wanchura back then, it seems Werner Transportation Co. had a lot of vehicles built "tough." This Autocar was owned by the operator. Note the four steps on the bumper, fender, cab, and top of cab used by the driver to climb up to the platform on the roof of the cab to check the reefer unit on the Brown trailer. Werner colors were red and gray. *Joe Wanchura*

Sterling trucks, such as this one, were very popular with the western freight haulers. Mojave Transportation Co. was transporting a load of bagged cement circa 1948. *Sterling Trucks*

Another popular truck among many of the carriers was this "WB" model White, pulling an Andrews trailer for Western Trucking Co. of St. Louis, Missouri. Note the shovel on the running board. *Western Trucking Co.*

Associated Transport Co. of New York City was one of the biggest trucking companies during the 1940s. The company owned the Brown Truck and Trailer Co., which constituted the entire fleet at this time. The Associated Transport trailer is a Fruehauf, and the Ward LaFrance tractor, having no logo, is probably a demo model on a tryout. *Ron Adams collection*

The owner of this 1947 Diamond T was F. H. Rysinger—who also owned Half Moon Express, which ran from Camden, New Jersey, to New York City in the late 1940s. The graphics, the company name, and the whitewall tires make for a real sharp-looking truck. *Joe Murphy*

Again, we see Half Moon Express in the spotlight with this early-1940s GMC Integral sleeper. This straight truck looks equally as good as the Half Moon Express Diamond T pictured on page 55. *Joe Murphy*

This circa 1948 Peterbilt and Brown body and pull-trailer was typical of the rigs used in the West. Note on the truck body the faint outline of the words Motor Express, Inc. This body, at one time, was probably mounted on a truck belonging to Los Angeles-Seattle Motor Express. *Portland-Seattle Auto Freight*

Reading Transportation Co. of Philadelphia was a smaller, regional company serving only Pennsylvania and New Jersey. This WB White was one of the power sources to pull the Strick trailer. *Reading Transportation Co.*

Another example of an unknown-make "create-your-own" truck. The truck was leased to Eastern Motor Express of Terre Haute, Indiana. The name "Lowells" on the gas tank was probably the owner. *Joe Wanchura*

This circa 1948 LJ Mack with a Trailmobile reefer trailer is a monster of a truck from the Midwest. The owner is unknown, but we do know that it was leased to Rowley Interstate, Inc. of Dubuque, Iowa. *Bob Ward*

This L model Mack and Fruehauf moving van was owned by Leonard Bros. Van and Storage Co. in Detroit, Michigan. It proudly wore the Allied Van Lines colors of orange and black. *Neil Sherff*

On the West Coast, a lot of these truck-trailer combinations could be seen in several different variations. This box truck and trailer was owned by West Coast Fast Freight of Seattle, Washington. This circa 1948 Sterling was a popular truck for western carriers. *Ernest Sternberg*

Harris Express, Inc. of Charlotte, North Carolina, ran up and down the East Coast from Georgia and the Carolinas into New Jersey and New York City. This late-1940s WB White and Black Diamond trailer was one of the many trucks in the Harris Express fleet. *Black Diamond Trailer Co.*

Another truck-trailer combination is this 1948 Kenworth with removable side body and pull-trailer. This unit was run throughout the Southwest by Western Truck Lines of Los Angeles. The company elected to add a sleeper box to this unit. *Western Truck Lines*

Fleetline, Inc. of Las Vegas, Nevada, had approximately 100 units running straight as an arrow overnight, every night, between Las Vegas and Los Angeles. One of those units was this circa 1947 Diamond T and Pike trailer. Fleetline was known as a pioneer trucker of the Southwest. *Joe Wanchura*

Another Diamond T, circa 1947, was this White's Transportation rig located somewhere in California. This set of flatbed doubles looks like a load of skids of wood. Corner angles helped secure the load and keep it together. *Ron Adams collection*

Produce was a popular commodity to haul up and down the Pacific Coast. Interstate Produce Express joined the ranks with this 1948 Peterbilt and Brown trailer. By this time, Peterbilt had gone from the four holes in the bumper to the four-line design. *Ron Adams collection*

Kenworth Trucks, such as this one, were very popular on the western trucking scene. The Fireball emblem on the hood tells us that it was Cummins powered. Post Transportation Co. of Carson, California, used this tank trailer to haul liquid corrosives for Stauffer Industrial Chemicals. *Steve Collins Photography*

Like many of the western companies, West Coast Fast Freight of Seattle had a variety of makes of trucks in its fleet. This Kenworth tractor and Fruehauf trailer was one of many in the fleet covering the Pacific Coast states in the late 1940s. *The Whittington Collection, California State University Long Beach*

Although this picture was taken in 1968 at Flemming Truck Stop in Carlisle, Pennsylvania, this 1949 LJ Mack was still doing its thing almost 20 years after it was made. Coldway Food Express of Sidney, Ohio, had this truck leased to it and pulled this Highway reefer trailer. *Ron Adams collection*

Truck-trailer combinations were used to haul almost any kind of freight. In this case, livestock is the cargo. Freitas Livestock Hauling in Stockton, California, was the owner of this late-1940s Kenworth. *Kenworth Truck Co.*

Truck-trailer combinations were not only made for conventional trucks but also for cab-over-engine models. This rare Sterling cab-over-engine was owned by Los Angeles-Seattle Motor Express. *Ernest Sternberg*

H. Sneath was the owner of this 1949 Diamond T. The truck was operated for Merchants Freight System of Terre Haute, Indiana, operating in an eight-state area. This one is pulling a Fruehauf stainless steel trailer. *Joe Wanchura*

There were a number of unusual-looking trucks traveling the American highways back in the 1940s. ARCO Auto Carriers of Chicago was the owner of this homemade truck with a Ford cab. The cargo of automobiles also happens to be Fords. *Joe Wanchura*

Bush Transfer, Inc. of Lenoir, North Carolina, was a new furniture hauler back in the 1940s. The job was done by using this model 154 Brockway and Black Diamond open-top furniture van trailer. *Black Diamond Trailer Co.*

Five Chevrolet tractors and five Highway trailers owned by Claude Parrish of Lincoln, Nebraska, were used to haul candy for Russell Stover Candies, also of Lincoln. Some of the loads were delivered to Hess Bros. Department Store in Allentown, Pennsylvania. *Ed Holm and Blomgren Photography*

Transcon Lines, Inc. of Los Angeles operated throughout the southwestern states. This 1949 Kenworth and Brown trailer was one in the fleet. The tractor was powered by a Cummins Diesel (notice the fireball Cummins Diesel decal on its side). *Kenworth Truck Co.*

Many specialized refrigerated carriers were based in Texas. Frozen Food Express of Dallas was one of the many companies that hauled meat and other refrigerated products from Texas to other parts of the country. F. A. Cowart was the owner of this 1949 GMC Model 750 and Brown reefer trailer. *Bill Wood Photo*

I-C-X, or Illinois California Express, was one of four Denver-based companies covering routes through the Southwest, the plains states, and into Chicago. The forerunner of this company was known as Los Angeles Albuquerque Express. Equipment such as this circa 1949 Kenworth and Brown trailer was common in the I-C-X operation from Denver to the West Coast. *Illinois California Express*

Many people think that Freightliner made only cab-over-engine (COE) trucks. Although every COE truck it manufactured before 1949 was used only in the Consolidated Freightways fleet. It did make a few conventional Freightliners, such as this one in 1949. It was used in Consolidated Freightway's heavy hauling division. Why it discontinued making these conventional tractors is unknown. The tractor's appearance was not bad looking at all. *Freightliner Corp.*

Consolidated Freight Lines, later known as Consolidated Copperstate Lines before it became Consolidated Freightways, ran between Los Angeles, Phoenix, and Tucson. This late-1940s Sterling with Fruehauf trailer was one of the trucks that traveled that route. Note the turn signals of that era. *Consolidated Freight Lines*

Spector Motor Service was one of the bigger trucking companies in 1949. With a home office in Chicago, Spector covered the Midwest states and into New England. This 1949 White 3000 and Bartlett trailer is shown at the Chicago Terminal after a relay run from Newark, Ohio. *Schube-Soucek Photography*

Consolidated Freightways of Menlo Park, California, took delivery of a fleet of brand-new Brown trailers in the mid- to late 1950s. Pulling the new trailer is the old 1949 Freightliner tractor. In the background, we can see one of the older C.F. trailers with the green shading, used into the later 1950s. To the left is one of the Ford Safety Vehicles that C.F. used. *Brown Trailers*

This late-1949 Peterbilt rigging tractor is loading oil field equipment on a flat-deck trailer in the oil fields of southern California. All the equipment was there to do the on-site-loading job. Lacey Trucking Co. of Long Beach was a heavy hauler and an oil field rigging company. *Inman Co.*

A tractor hauling heavy, oversized loads always got attention going down the highway. Leonard Bros. Transfer Co. of Miami, Florida, had the honors of moving this large test chamber from New York to Texas. An REO tractor and Talbert TD-40-RG-RA model trailer accomplished the mission. *Leonard Bros. Transfer Co.*

This photo, we can say, represents pairs. First, we have two Autocar tractors. The one on the left is a C50T; on the right is a C70T, both on 148-inch wheelbases. The tractors are pulling two matching 32-foot Fruehauf trailers. Schneiders Transfer of Richmond, Virginia, hauls for two firms, Atlantic and Pacific Tea Co. and the Virginia Alcoholic Beverage Control Board. Notice that the C50T has round gas tanks and the C70T has saddle tanks. *Autocar Trucks*

CHAPTER FIVE
DECADE OF CONSOLIDATION IN THE 1950S

Two things that came into being in the 1950s were piggybacking and the planning of our current interstate highway system. Piggybacking was the practice of putting semi-trailers on the railroad flatcars and railing them across country. This move took work away from truck drivers.

Our interstate highway system was designed around 1951, although actual construction didn't start until 1956. This highway network, known as the National Defense Highway System, not only benefited travelers, but the trucking industry as well. Travel and delivery time were cut considerably because trucks could bypass the big cities instead of having to travel through many towns and deal with the stop-and-go traffic lights.

By the time 1950 rolled around, truck manufacturers settled back into their usual competitive development battles. White and GMC started off the postwar one-upmanship

Picking up or delivering freight was not only done in local towns but also at ports. This 1950s-era Freightliner truck-trailer combination for Consolidated Freightways, Inc. waits beside a huge cargo ship for a pickup. *Consolidated Freightways*

Many companies usually stuck with the same brand names of trucks and trailers. This is a Peterbilt tractor of the early 1950s and a Brown 40-foot trailer for Pacific Intermountain Express Co. The longer wheelbase tractors were used west of Denver because the length laws allowed them. Notice that there is very little chrome on the P-I-E vehicles. *Pacific Intermountain Express*

with a new model and cab design in the late 1940s. International introduced its new L series and the new L series cab-over-engine Emeryville in 1950. When one manufacturer came out with a new model, everyone else had to follow suit. Kenworth came out with its newly redesigned cab-over-engine that came to be known as the popular Bullnose. Peterbilt introduced its Bubblenose cab-over. Mack came out with the new A series.

Throughout the 1950s, truck manufacturers continued to refine and improve their models. Mack had the W-71, International had the Cherrypicker, and GMC had the Cannonball.

In 1951, the White Motor Co. took over the manufacturing operations of the Sterling Motor Truck Co. and changed the name to Sterling White. White also changed its name when White and Freightliner signed a 25-year agreement to sell Freightliner trucks through White dealerships, provided that Freightliner would add the name White to its trucks. This was the birth of the White-Freightliner.

In the later 1950s, the manufacturers went to the flat-front cabs. Among those flat-front models that stood out were the International DCO series Emeryville. Mack also came out with the "G" series flat-front cab, and then in 1957 introduced the B67 (a conventional tractor and not a cab-over-engine type), which had the concave cab.

All the truck makers that made cab-over-engine models went to the flat-front cabs. In 1956, International went to the DCO Series, known as the Emeryville. In 1958, Mack started the "G" series. Kenworth, Freightliner, and Peterbilt started their flat-front COEs around 1955. The COE models had bigger windshields for better vision, and as previous COEs had been, they were offered in sleeper versions or just day cabs. They also offered a variety of diesel engines. One of the popular ones was the 220 horsepower Cummins Diesel.

At the same time, 40-foot trailers became the norm in order to make hauling more payload possible. The flat-front COEs came in a variety of wheelbases. The wheelbase you could use depended on what part of the country you were located in. In the western states, wheelbases went as long as 240 to 260 inches. In the eastern part of the country, the allowable wheelbase depended a lot on the length of the trailer being pulled. And with the ongoing construction of the new interstate highway system, more freight was hauled farther and faster by truck than ever before. Around 1960, on the Ohio, Indiana, and Massachusetts turnpikes and the New York State Thruway, carriers were able to pull double 40-foot trailers. Once the double-40s reached the end of the turnpike, they were separated into single 40s to continue to their final destination.

Trucking companies were also on the move in the 1950s, with mergers and buyouts becoming common. In two of the biggest mergers, Pacific Intermountain Express Co. (P-I-E) of Oakland, California, took over the operations of West Coast Fast Freight of Seattle; and Consolidated Freightways, Inc. of Menlo Park, California, took over the operations of the Motor Cargo Co. of Akron, Ohio. This latter move made C.F. the second coast-to-coast carrier.

Other significant mergers included Spector Motor Service and Mid-States Freight Lines, both of Chicago. Western Truck Lines of Los Angeles merged with Gillette Motor Transport of Dallas. Another Dallas outfit, Strickland Transportation Co. Inc., merged with Kelleher Motor Freight Lines of Chicago. Johnson Motor Lines and Atlantic States Motor Lines combined during this period, as did Mason and Dixon Lines and Silver Fleet Motor Express, and Norwalk Truck Lines and Shirks Motor Express.

After the war-hampered decade of the 1940s, the 1950s was a time of progressive change for truck manufacturers and trucking companies alike. This pattern would continue into the 1960s with a number of big expansion moves that created some trucking giants.

This 32 Series tractor was used in the western operations for Consolidated Freightways. It was the first integral sleeper introduced by Freightliner in 1950. The tire chains were always there to combat the winter snowstorms in the mountains of Oregon, Washington, and Idaho. *Freightliner Corp.*

Savage Transportation Co. of San Francisco was a common carrier that ran between Los Angeles and San Francisco. This 1950 Model 280 cab-over-engine Peterbilt and Fruehauf double trailers are waiting for the ship to come in at the docks. *Ron Adams collection*

This Peterbilt tractor and Trailmobile trailer were part of a mixed group of brands of tractors and trailers in the Navajo Freight Lines' fleet. A number of trucking companies used an Indian as their insignia, with Navajo being a more popular one. *Navajo Freight Lines, Inc.*

The flying wing wheel was the symbol of fast service for ET & WNC Transportation Co. of Johnson City, Tennessee, which operated in the Carolinas and Tennessee. This 1950 WC White with Black Diamond trailer was among about 140 tractors in the orange, white, and black fleet of ET & WNC. *Black Diamond Trailer Co.*

Moving this big Bucyrus Erie shovel was the order of the day for Owl Truck Co. of Compton, California. What looks like it could be a really big job was probably just another day's work for an experienced hauler like Owl. A Mack tractor pulled the 75-ton Utility low-bed trailer. This Mack was probably a homemade truck, modified to Owl's engineering. It also had several modified Peterbilts. This is certainly not an off-the-shelf Mack. *Utility Trailers*

Garrett Freightlines, Inc. of Pocatello, Idaho, operated in 11 western states. This circa 1951 Kenworth was Cummins powered and pulled a Williamsen van-trailer. Garrett's colors were a colorful yellow and green. *Garrett Freightlines, inc.*

Though many trucking companies used simple graphics and common colors to display their names, there were carriers like Sites Freightlines, Inc. of Portland, Oregon, (formerly Portland-Pendleton Transport) that believed in bold and bright colors and graphics. The Kenworth tractor and Utility trailer are decked out in their Sunday best for traveling on the Oregon highways. *Sites Freightlines, Inc.*

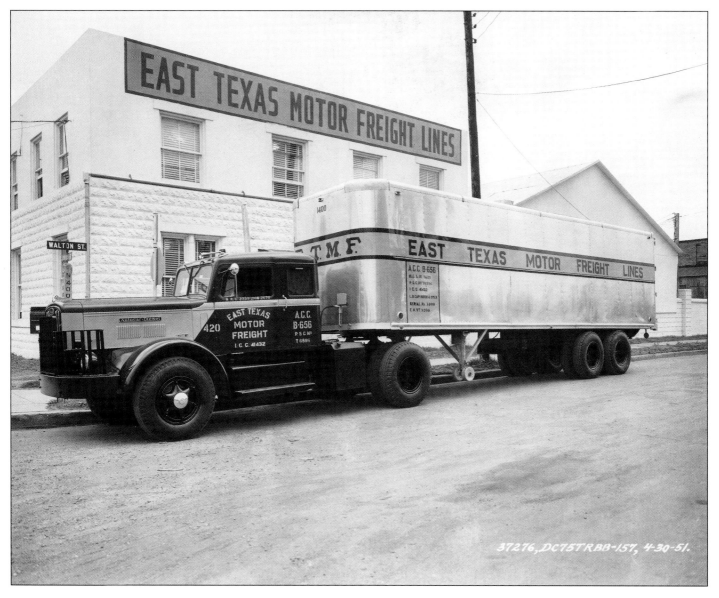

April 30, 1954, was picture day for this four-wheeled piece of "Big Iron." If any truck came on looking like a mean machine, this DC-75 Autocar sleeper was the one. Autocar always built tough and ready-looking trucks. East Texas Motor Freight Lines of Dallas, Texas, was proud to have this truck operating in its fleet. *Autocar Trucks*

Sleeper cabs like this 650 GMC were popular with some companies. The post-exterior trailer is a Fruehauf-Carter. McLean Trucking Co. of Winston-Salem, North Carolina, used this GMC sleeper to run up and down the East Coast. *Carter McLean Trucking Co.*

One of the bigger eastern companies was Spector Motor Service of Chicago, whose territory ranged from Missouri across the Midwest and into New England. Trucks such as this White 3000 with Fruehauf trailer was used throughout their system. *Spector Motor Service*

Florida palm trees make up the background for this White 3000 sleeper and Great Dane furniture van, both circa 1951. Boasting 50 years of dependable service, Delcher Moving & Storage of Jacksonville, Florida, got its start around 1900. *Delcher Moving & Storage*

Another tough and ready Autocar was the DC75. Charles Kendziers is the proud owner of truck L-606. He hails from Sutton, Massachusetts. Kendziers leased his truck to Associated Transport of New York City. A Fireball Cummins plate tells us that the truck is Cummins powered. *Autocar Trucks*

Republic Van Lines of Los Angeles, California, was a cross-country household goods transporter. This 1952 REO with Utility furniture van is typical of the type of trucks that were used in this business. *REO Motor Co.*

Pilot Freight Carriers of Winston-Salem, North Carolina, was one of the larger southern carriers that ran up into the Northeast. This 1952-era White 3000 sleeper and Strick trailer is typical of the equipment Pilot ran at this time. Note the picture in the sleeper window. *Pilot Freight Carriers*

Freight carriers come in all sizes, from as few as 5 or 10 trucks to well over 3,000. Russ Phillips Trucking of Fresno, California, was far from being one of the larger carriers, but handled its small operation the same as the large carriers did. Phillips took pride in its equipment by keeping it well maintained, as shown here with this early-1950s Peterbilt Bubblenose tractor and Fruehauf reefer trailer. *Brian Williams*

These Kenworth Bullnose and Williamsen double trailers are part of the Garrett Freight Lines fleet. Notice the whitewall tires around the whole rig. Try to imagine the Garrett colors of green and yellow on this truck against the western scenery background. It would make for a rather colorful setting. *Garrett Freightlines, inc.*

In 1951, the White Motor Co. took over the operations of the Sterling Motor Truck Co., changing the name to Sterling White. This is a 1952 Cleveland-built Sterling White owned by the Main Trucking & Rigging Co. of Paterson, New Jersey. Since the Sterling White is a 1952 model, one might think that the Army tank is being hauled for the Korean War. Not so, since the plate on the bumper shows the photo was taken in 1964. *Main Trucking & Rigging Co.*

In the 1950s, Canadian trucks were basically the same as the American trucks. This 1952 Model WF-64T White Freightliner with Brown trailer was traveling the western Canada highways for Continental Carriers, Ltd. of Vancouver, British Columbia. *Ron Adams collection*

The sign on the front of the tractor reads "Long Load"-loads don't come much longer than this. Not only is it a long load, but the White Freightliner tractor is also on a long wheelbase. Hauling loads like this looks like a really big job, but to a specialized carrier like St. Johns Motor Express of Portland, Oregon, it's routine. *Ackroyd Photography, Inc.*

Harris Express, Inc. of Charlotte, North Carolina, operated from the Carolinas up the East Coast into New Jersey and New York City. W. P. Beaver was the owner of this circa 1953 LJ Mack and Fruehauf trailer. *Harris Express, Inc.*

In the mid-1950s, International made huge cab-over-engine tractors such as this RD model for over-the-road hauling. Eastern Motor Express, Inc. of Terre Haute, Indiana, proudly displays its name and all the cities it serves on the Fruehauf "Road Star" trailer. *Eastern Motor Express, Inc.*

Carriers often interlined in order to offer better and more complete service. This shows Ringsby Truck Lines, Inc. of Denver interlining with Inland Freight Lines of Salt Lake City, Utah, around 1953. Later on, Inland Freight Lines did become part of the Ringsby Truck Lines operation. Peterbilt tractors and Williamsen trailers were part of a mixed bag of equipment. *Ringsby Truck Lines, Inc.*

Omaha, Nebraska, was the home office of Watson Bros. Transportation Co. The Watson routes went from Chicago to the Rockies, the Southwest, and into California. Since Watson Bros. had a lot of lease operators, their equipment, such as this circa 1953 dual-stick Bubblenose Peterbilt and Brown trailer, made for a sharp-looking fleet of trucks. *Watson Bros. Transportation Co.*

The orange, black, and white trucks for ET & WNC Transportation Co. of Johnson City, Tennessee, could be seen traveling the highways through Tennessee and the Carolinas. The 1953 vintage "WC" White and Black Diamond trailer was one combination in its growing fleet. *Black Diamond Trailer Co.*

North State Motor Lines, Inc. of Rocky Mount, North Carolina, used this circa 1953 WC White and Dorsey trailer for hauling grain. Notice the two small access doors on the side of the trailer for side unloading. *Dorsey Trailer Co.*

Transporting liquids often required special engineering—tankers must be engineered and designed according to what liquid would be hauled. Colonial Tank Transport of New Brunswick, New Jersey, was a bulk hauler. This WC White is pulling a tank trailer designed for a specific liquid commodity. *Fred Keesing Photography*

Highway Express Lines of Philadelphia plied the routes of eastern Pennsylvania. The cargo on this trip was Budweiser beer. A WC White and Strick trailer delivered the cargo to its destination. *White Motor Co.*

Signs of some inclement weather was not enough to stop this LJ Mack and Black Diamond trailer from making its delivery for Hennis Freight Lines of Winston-Salem, North Carolina. *Neil Sherff*

Some of the equipment that was run in eastern Canada was similar to ours here in the eastern United States. Wallace Transport, Ltd. used this Diamond T to pull the open-top rack-side trailer for this trip. *Ron Adams collection*

Typical of western equipment is this long wheelbase circa 1953 White Freightliner. Arrowhead Freightlines of Salt Lake City used this combination to cover its territory between Salt Lake City and southern California. *White Motor Co.*

Many produce and reefer trucking companies ran out of Florida. Miles Trucking Co. of Plant City, Florida, used this circa 1953 LJ Mack sleeper and Fruehauf reefer trailer. The produce arrived at its destination on time and fresh. *Harry Patterson*

"Now joining the North and South" was the motto for Mason and Dixon Lines of Kingsport, Tennessee. This 1953 White 3000 and Fruehauf Road Star trailer were one rig in a whole fleet of the same. Mason and Dixon covered Georgia, Tennessee, the Carolinas, and Virginia into the mid-Atlantic states. *Pierce Studios*

Kingsway Transport, Ltd. of Montreal, Quebec. Its territory at this time covered Ontario, Quebec, and down into New Jersey and New York. This 1953 LJ Mack with Fruehauf trailer was one in a fleet of 292 tractors and 435 trailers. *Arnott and Rogers Photography*

If you traveled between Philadelphia and New York City, you could see this C-65-T Autocar and Fruehauf trailer making its way to or from Philadelphia for Blue Comet Express. Joseph Braun was the owner of the fleet of 23 tractors and 33 trailers. *Autocar Trucks*

This circa 1953 Bullnose Kenworth and Aero-Liner reefer trailer may have been one of the sharpest-looking rigs on the road west of Chicago at the time. This showpiece includes four air horns, dual stacks, air conditioner, five bullet cab lights, extra rear-view-clearance mirrors, two antennas, sun visor, and an oversize sleeper box. The name Midwest Coast Transport, Inc. of Minneapolis, also stands out. M.C.T. ran from the Midwestern states to the West Coast. Their colors were black and green with a white stripe. *Ron Adams collection*

The blue-and-orange trucks of Miller Motor Express of Charlotte, North Carolina, ran from Atlanta up the Atlantic Coast to New York City. This 1953 WC22 White with Great Dane trailer was from a fleet of 122 tractors and 133 trailers among 14 terminals. *Miller Motor Express*

This H60T Mack "Cherrypicker" and Fruehauf trailer stopped long enough for a picture in November 1953. Dixie Highway Express of Meridian, Mississippi, had a fleet of 150 tractors and 300 trailers among 13 terminals in Georgia, Alabama, Mississippi, and Louisiana. *Mack Trucks*

These gray and black trucks for Time Freight, Inc. of Lubbock, Texas, could be seen making their way from California to Tennessee and through the Southwest. This WC 2462 White and Utility trailer was one unit in the fleet of 91 tractors and 133 trailers. The tractor had a pusher axle that was dead, but was made alive by a belt powered by the rear drive axle. *White Motor Co.*

The yellow-and-green trucks of Denver-Amarillo Express of Amarillo, Texas, ran among 9 terminals in Texas, Colorado, and New Mexico. Although not very large, this WC 24 White with Fruehauf trailer was part of a fleet of 40 tractors and 98 trailers. *J. Howard Miller, Photographer*

Healy Motor Lines was a small company operating in Texas and four surrounding states out of Fort Worth. Although its main hauling was for oil field equipment, it did have a few livestock trucks. This 3000 White sleeper with what could be a Hyde trailer was one of the units. *Healy Motor Lines*

Milne Truck Lines of St. George was a small company in Utah. A fleet of 12 tractors and 37 trailers covered four Utah terminals. This Kenworth with Dromedary box and Utility trailer was one of the fleet. Dromedary rigs were common in the western states. *Milne Truck Lines*

"The Only Coast-to-Coast Carrier" was seen for many years emblazoned on the trailers of the Denver-Chicago Trucking Co. of Denver, Colorado. That slogan started in 1946 when Denver-Chicago bought out the Adams Transfer and Storage Co. of Kansas City, Missouri, giving Denver-Chicago Adams' rights east of Chicago. This circa 1954 Kenworth with Timpte trailer was in the fleet of various makes of 398 tractors and 753 trailers stationed among 14 terminals. *Denver-Chicago Trucking Co.*

Kramer Bros. Freight Lines, Inc. of Detroit covered an area from Chicago to New York City, as can be seen on the side of the trailer. This 1954 DC-75 Autocar was owned by Harry Mentzer of Baltimore, and it pulled a Trailmobile open-top trailer 32 feet long. *Autocar Trucks*

W. T. Cowan Fast Freight of Baltimore used a total of 152 tractors and 218 trailers to run between Baltimore and New York City. This black-and-green 1954 C65T Autocar and Fruehauf Carter trailer was one of the fleet. *Autocar Trucks*

Around 1954, a four-car auto hauler was the biggest that could be found in the East. In the West, it was a different story. As shown in this photo, six cars would be hauled at one time. Western Auto Transport, Inc. of Denver used this mid-1950s Kenworth cab-over to haul these Rambler, DeSoto, and Plymouth cars. *Hal Rumel Photography*

Truck-trailer combinations were common in the West. Garibaldi Bros. of Los Angeles used this circa 1954 Kenworth with Fruehauf body and pull-trailer to haul livestock. They had a total of 80 rigs hauling livestock in Arizona, California, Idaho, Nevada, New Mexico, Oregon, and Utah. *Kenworth Truck Co.*

"Through the Great Southwest" was the slogan of Albuquerque-Phoenix Express of Albuquerque, New Mexico. The red-and-yellow trucks, such as this circa 1954 LTL Mack and Fruehauf trailer, were part of the small Apex fleet of 10 tractors and 15 trailers. *C. E. Redman*

Lee & Eastes, Inc. of Seattle not only had a dry freight operation but also a special commodities division and a bulk petroleum division. This circa 1954 White Freightliner with Fruehauf trailer was among the fleet of 40 tractors and 45 trailers. *Lee & Eastes, Inc.*

Denver was the main hub for four of the bigger trucking companies, including Navajo Freight Lines, Inc. Before the name was changed to Navajo, the company was known as Kansas City-Los Angeles Flyer Transport. Navajo routes ran through the Southwest, north to Denver and east to St. Louis and Chicago. The main office was in Albuquerque, New Mexico, before it was moved to Denver. The DC-100 Autocar and Fruehauf trailer were in the fleet of 165 tractors and 419 trailers. *White Motor Co.*

Gordons Transport, Inc. of Memphis, Tennessee, used this 1956 International and Fruehauf trailer throughout its system. The fleet was made up of 195 tractors and 297 trailers. *Gordons Transport, Inc.*

Riss & Company had a whole fleet of these Cannonball-cab GMCs and Fruehauf-Carter trailers. Based in Kansas City, Missouri, Riss terminals stretched from Denver to Boston. The fleet at this time totaled 500 tractors, 1,000 trailers, and 400 reefers. "Express Service at Freight Rates" was its famous slogan. *Eaton Corp.*

Many companies seemed to cover the territory from Chicago to New York City and Boston. Among them was Mid-States Freight Lines of Chicago, founded by Cecil Vernon in the 1930s. Among the 800 units in the fleet was this B65LT Mack and Brown trailer. *Mack Trucks*

The Jack Cole Co. of Birmingham, Alabama, operated from Alabama to Ohio, Indiana, and Michigan. This 860 GMC Cannonball was one of 169 tractors, and the Trailmobile trailer was one of 274 in the fleet. Jack Cole Co. and Dixie Highway Express became part of Admiral Merchants Freight System. *Jimmy Wilson Studio*

The Arizona cactus scenery makes a nice background for a company like Texas-Arizona Motor Freight of El Paso, Texas. The T-A trucks ran from Los Angeles to El Paso. This Kenworth tractor and Trailmobile trailer were one of 94 rigs in the fleet. *Texas-Arizona Motor Freight*

Shirks Motor Express, Inc. of Lancaster, Pennsylvania, covered an area between northern New Jersey and Cleveland, Ohio, with a fleet of 219 tractors and 555 trailers scattered among 15 terminals. One of the units was this circa 1956 H-63 Mack and Fruehauf trailer. *Peels Studios*

The tall brother to the H-63 Mack is the H-61 Mack, known as the Cherrypicker because of the high cab. S&W Motor Lines, Inc. of Greensboro, North Carolina, had this H-61 Mack and flatbed trailer loaded with mixed freight somewhere in Michigan. Not a very large company at the time, S&W had a fleet of 37 tractors and 45 trailers hauling among 19 states. *Neil Sherff*

Willig Freight Lines, Inc. ran from its home base in San Francisco to Los Angeles. Willig had a variety of equipment in a fleet of 50 tractors and 98 trailers. This H-61 Mack with a Reliance Dromedary body and Trailmobile trailer was a typical Willig western unit. *Willig Freight Lines*

In the mid-1950s, Alterman Transport Lines ran trucks like this circa 1955 R-200 International and Great Dane reefer trailer throughout the eastern half of the United States. *Kaye-Lu Photographers*

Though Merchants Fast Motor Lines of Abilene, Texas, only covered one state, it was still a sizable carrier because of the size of Texas. Merchants had 43 terminals scattered statewide, from El Paso to Dallas and down to Houston. The fleet included 156 tractors and 223 trailers, including this circa 1955 White 9000 and Fruehauf trailer. *Merchants Fast Motor Lines*

Louisville, Kentucky, was the home office of the Silver Fleet Motor Express Co. A nine-state area from Illinois to Tennessee and the Carolinas was covered with a fleet of 615 pieces of equipment. This 9000 White was painted blue and silver and pulled a Fruehauf trailer. Silver Fleet was later purchased and became part of the Mason and Dixon Lines System of Kingsport, Tennessee. *Silver Fleet Motor Express, Co.*

Eastern Motor Express of Terre Haute, Indiana, was one of the biggest companies in the mid-1950s. Terminals were located in 19 major cities from St. Louis to Jersey City, New Jersey. The fleet of 450 tractors and 650 trailers included all makes, among them this H-61 Mack Cherrypicker and Fruehauf reefer trailer. *Eastern Motor Express*

In the mid-1950s, Kenworth, like other truck manufacturers, restyled its cab-over-engine tractors from the Bullnose-cab to the flat-front cab. This Kenworth tractor was leased to the refrigerated division of Ringsby Truck Lines, Inc. of Denver, Colorado, by a lease operator whose name is believed to be R. E. Hakeworth. Both the tractor and the Trailmobile reefer trailer are perfect examples of western-style rigs of the 1950s. *Ringsby Truck Lines, Inc.*

From farm to dairy to store-this was the routine for raw milk. Robert H. Carr & Sons of Frazer, Pennsylvania, hauled it to the dairy. The B42 Mack and the Heil tanker make for a nice combination and did the job well. *Robert H. Carr & Sons*

Carolina Freight Carriers, Inc. of Cherryville, North Carolina, had a long chain of terminals that stretched from Tampa, Florida, to Boston. The 288-tractor and 391-trailer fleet comprised a variety of makes, including this big Ford cab-over-engine and Great Dane reefer trailer photographed at the Philadelphia terminal. *Robert J. Parrish*

Known as the "Sidewinder," this cab-beside-engine (CBE) cab style was introduced by Kenworth in 1955. This cab was not used by many companies, although it served its purpose of cutting down on weight. Yellow Transit Freight Lines of Kansas City, Missouri, used some of these along its routes from Amarillo and Houston, Texas, up to Chicago. The fleet of 312 tractors and 500 trailers were stationed among 19 terminals. *Yellow Transit Freight Lines*

Another Kenworth CBE, this one a sleeper version, was used by the Buckingham Transportation Co. of Rapid City, South Dakota. The company operated in Minnesota, Iowa, the Dakotas, Nebraska, Colorado, Wyoming, and Montana. The Brown reefer trailer and Kenworth tractor were part of the fleet of 160 tractors. Buckingham merged with United Truck Lines and became known as United-Buckingham Freight System. *Buckingham Transportation Co.*

On August 6, 1955, this White 3000 and Strick trailer stopped long enough for a photo. Davidson Transfer and Storage Co. of Baltimore operated between Richmond, Virginia, and New York City. The fleet comprised 194 tractors and 277 trailers. *McLaughlin Bros.*

Multiple license plates and permit numbers were common on all trucks in the past. Aero Mayflower Transit Co. of Indianapolis, Indiana, moved household goods in this circa 1955 big RD International Cherrypicker with a Trailmobile moving van. *Robert J. Parrish*

Illinois-California Express of Denver had a number of the Kenworth CBE Sidewinder cabs. A total of 15 terminals stretched from Chicago to Denver, through the Southwest into Los Angeles. With both cab-over-engine and conventional tractors in the fleet, there were 141 tractors and 220 trailers. *Illinois-California Express*

Portland-Pendleton Transport of Portland, Oregon, also used the Kenworth Sidewinder. Like many of the companies from the Pacific Northwest, they weren't very large. But the services they offered were equal to those of the larger carriers. The Kenworth CBE and the Utility double trailers were painted in a rather striking color scheme of black, yellow, green, and blue. Portland-Pendleton later became Sites Freight Lines. *Kenworth Truck Co.*

Arizona-Nevada Express of Phoenix was a small southwestern carrier running between Phoenix and Las Vegas. This "Roadrunner" fleet had 35 units. The circa 1955 Kenworth CBE and Kingham double trailers shown here made this run. *Arizona-Nevada Express*

Knaus Truck Lines of Kansas City, Missouri, was another of the many companies that operated between Denver and Chicago. A fleet of 89 tractors, such as this mid-1950s RD International, and 152 trailers, such as this Fruehauf van, hauled freight among 10 terminals in 6 Midwestern states. *Knaus Truck Lines*

Pacific Intermountain Express Co. (P-I-E) of Oakland, California, was one of the top 10 trucking companies over the years. In 1955, P-I-E had a fleet of 334 tractors and 620 trailers. At this time, the company had taken over the operations of West Coast Fast Freight of Seattle, Washington, which gave P-I-E an additional 228 tractors and 404 trailers for a total fleet of 562 tractors and 1,024 trailers. This RD International and Fruehauf reefer was one in the P-I-E fleet. The two operations gave P-I-E authority to cover the West Coast, Rocky Mountain states, and into Chicago. *Pacific Intermountain Express Co.*

Akron, Ohio, was the home office of All States Freight, Inc., with routes from Chicago to Boston. A total of 375 tractors and 450 trailers made up the fleet. In 1965 P-I-E took over the operations of All States Freight, Inc. A B-61 Mack and Trailmobile trailer are parked in front of the main office. *All States Freight, Inc.*

Though Western Trucking Company of St. Louis only had three terminals, they were in Cincinnati, St. Louis, and Louisville, and the company was large enough to require a fleet of 125 tractors and 175 trailers. The tandem-axle, belt-drive White 3000 and Kentucky trailer were part of the fleet. *Western Trucking Co.*

Some of the western trucking companies came up with their own equipment configurations and design. Ringsby Truck Lines of Denver, known as the "Line of The Rockets," used this unusual configuration in 1956. The White-Freightliner and Utility trailers were one unit in a fleet of 131 tractors and 177 trailers that traveled from the West Coast east into Chicago. *Freightliner Corp.*

Livestock hauling was big business in the Midwest. Murphy Transportation Co. of Hampton, Iowa, used an all-GMC tractor fleet like this one with a Dorsey open-top livestock trailer. *Murphy Transportation Co.*

Perhaps the biggest trucking company in the 1950s was Interstate Motor Freight System of Grand Rapids, Michigan. This DC-75 Autocar with Highway trailer are one unit in this large fleet of 775 tractors and 950 trailers. E. S. Timmerman was the owner of the tractor. Interstate route authority stretched from St. Paul and St. Louis to Boston. *Autocar Trucks*

Garrett Freightlines had a network of 35 terminals throughout the 11 western states. These H-60 Mack and Williamsen open-top double trailers are among the types of units in the mixed fleet. *Garrett Freightlines*

Paper Transport of Wilmington, Delaware, had a sharp-looking fleet of trucks. The colors were black and green with white pinstriping, the latter reportedly done by a state trooper in Delaware. Clifford Sparks is the owner of the company. This H-63 Mack and Gindy open-top trailer are nice-looking trucks. *Robert J. Parrish*

This circa 1956 Kenworth with Fruehauf trailer was used by C. R. England & Sons of Salt Lake City, Utah, to haul produce across the country in the 1950s. *Neil Sherff*

Grey Van Lines, an affiliate of Greyhound Bus Lines, was a household goods carrier with a variety of tractors in the fleet. The R Series International with Fruehauf trailer is ready to move someone into a new home. *Grey Van Lines*

This unique 1956 Peterbilt with a Dromedary and Trailmobile trailer could haul a lot of freight for Ringsby. The Cummins diesel was located underneath the frame behind the twin steering axles. The sleeper was located high above the cab. *Ringsby Truck Lines, Inc.*

Watkins Motor Lines of Thomasville, Georgia, was one of the biggest refrigerated haulers operating in the eastern half of the country in the mid-1950s. Nine terminals serviced a fleet of 135 tractors and 150 trailers. The B-73 Mack was owned by Gene Hyde and leased to Watkins. *Neil Sherff*

The black and orange trucks of H. R. Cook Truck Lines of Jonesboro, Arkansas, could be seen traveling from the South to the Great Lakes states. This RD Series International and Great Dane trailer made up one of the rigs operating in this area. Notice the six-point star of the front wheel. *Neil Sherff*

Santa Fe Transportation Co. of Los Angeles was the trucking operation of the Santa Fe Railroad. The red-and-white RD International and Fruehauf trailer were among 67 road tractors and 119 road trailers in the fleet. *Santa Fe Railway*

This RD International with a Black Diamond trailer is owned by Bush Transfer, Inc. of Lenoir, North Carolina, owner of 16 tractors and 16 trailers. The operation ran from the Carolinas up the Atlantic Coast to New York City. *Robert J. Parrish*

The letters A, C, and E stand for the three cities where A.C.E. Transportation, Inc. started in the trucking business: Akron, Ohio, and Connersville and Evansville, Indiana. H. C. Hartline was the owner and founder of A.C.E. This B-42 Mack and Ohio trailer were owned by Max Rabel and leased to A.C.E. Transportation Co. in 1957. The truck, No. 501, was driven by Archie Follweiler. A total of 169 tractors and 202 trailers were in the fleet. *A.C.E. Transportation Co.*

Not one, but two stacks deck this DC-75 Autocar pulling a Fruehauf trailer owned by Bob Johnson of South Bend, Indiana. The rig is leased to Safeway Truck Lines of Chicago, which used a fleet of 180 tractor-trailer units to haul refrigerated products between Nebraska and Boston. *Robert J. Parrish*

This circa 1956 W-71 Mack and Fruehauf reefer trailer were also leased to Safeway Truck Lines. The W-71 Mack was made from 1953 to 1958. A total of 215 were produced. *Robert J. Parrish*

Mason and Dixon Lines of Kingsport, Tennessee, stayed with one make. This White 9000 was one of the many Whites the company had in its fleet over the years. Mason and Dixon was also a big user of Brown trailers. *Mason and Dixon Lines*

In 1956, Johnson Motor Lines of Charlotte, North Carolina, was an Atlantic Coast carrier. It also operated with Atlantic States Motor Lines. This DC 405-L International is one of the fleet of 206 tractors and 334 trailers. On the left is W. E. Hampton, president of United Equipment and Service, Inc.; on the right is M. E. Sheahan, president of Johnson Motor Lines. *Johnson Motor Lines*

Similar to the Twin Steer Dromedary used by Ringsby Truck Lines is this Twin Steer Kenworth with Brown Dromedary body and Brown trailer used by Pacific Intermountain Express, Inc. of Oakland, California. Rigs like this were used west of Denver due to length laws. P-I-E had a variety of different makes and types of equipment in the fleet of 562 tractors and 1,024 trailers. *Pacific Intermountain Express, Inc.*

In 1957, Spector Motor Service and Mid-States Freight Lines, Inc. of Chicago merged and became Spector Freight System, Inc., with a total of 1,935 tractors and trailers. The H-63 Mack and Brown trailer represents a sample of the sleeper equipment in the fleet. *Spector Freight System, Inc.*

Central Motor Lines of Charlotte, North Carolina, used this 1957 H-63 Mack to run from the Carolinas up the East Coast to New York City, and to Cleveland and Chicago in the Midwest. More than 800 pieces of equipment traveled between their terminals. *Central Motor Lines*

Livestock was far from the easiest kind of freight to haul. However, the cattle traveled in style in this Fruehauf trailer, hauled by a custom DC-100 Autocar with dual chrome stacks and a 60-inch aluminum sleeper. Owner A. H. "Jack" Dawson of Montana probably only had this one truck at the time. *Fruehauf Trailers*

This custom DC-100 Autocar was leased to Little Audrey's Transportation Co. of Fremont, Nebraska. The blue-and-white color scheme, dual chrome stacks, and lots of chrome extras made this truck the pride of the fleet. Little Audrey's was a refrigerated carrier hauling from the Midwestern states to the West Coast. *Autocar Trucks*

This White Freightliner for Los Angeles-Seattle Motor Express and Fruehauf trailer for Time Freight, Inc. are interlining in this 1956 photo. *Kelly-Holiday*

In another example of interlining, this big International RD West Coast tractor was owned by Navajo Freight Lines of Denver, and the Trailmobile trailer was probably owned by Kelleher Motor Freight Lines of St. Louis, (which was likely taken over temporarily by Strickland Transportation Co. of Dallas). Notice in the background a REO tractor, probably used as a city delivery tractor. *Mile High Photography*

Adley Express Co. of New Haven, Connecticut, provided service along the Atlantic Coast from Boston to Suffolk, Virginia, using equipment like this 1957 B-61 Mack and Strick trailer. *Adley Express Co.*

"Look For The Blue-Eyed Indian" was a slogan used on the Dromedary rigs in the western part of the Navajo Freight Lines operation. Dromedaries were not used east of Denver due to length laws. This 1957 International DCO Emeryville was one type of tractor used for Dromedary setups. A lot of western freight carriers used as much space as available to haul extra freight. *Ron Adams collection*

Kroblin Refrigerated Express, Inc., a refrigerated carrier based in Sumner, Iowa, had its own fleet of tractors, but shown here is a leased 1957 Diamond T pulling one of the company's Fruehauf reefer trailers. Kroblin hauled from the Midwestern states to the East Coast and New England area. *Neil Sherff*

This International DCO Emeryville with Trailmobile body and trailer was a twin-steering Dromedary nicknamed "Mr. Many Wheels" by the drivers. In 1957, the Navajo fleet totaled 790 trucks and 1,126 trailers. *Navajo Freight Lines, Inc.*

Ruke Transport Lines, Inc., a refrigerated carrier based out of Ft. Myers, Florida, covered the territory from Florida to Illinois and Michigan in the Midwest and up the East Coast to New York City. The H-63 Mack and Brown reefer trailer were leased to Ruke by W. R. Carter. *Neil Sherff*

W. T. Cowan Fast Freight, Inc. of Baltimore got this B-61 Mack tractor and Great Dane rack-side trailer dressed up in its black-and-green Sunday best for a photo on October 23, 1957. Some 152 tractors and 218 trailers made up the Cowan over-the-road fleet. *McLaughlin Bros.*

Little Audrey's Transportation Co. of Fremont, Nebraska, leased this 1957 Diamond T and Fruehauf reefer trailer. The company colors were blue and silver. Little Audrey's hauled from the Midwestern states to the Pacific Northwest and West Coast. *Neil Sherff*

Midwest Coast Transport, Inc. of Sioux Falls, South Dakota, was a refrigerated carrier hauling from the Midwest to the Pacific Northwest and West Coast. The owner-operator fleet included this 1957 W-71 Mack and Fruehauf reefer trailer. *Ron Adams collection*

Daniels Motor Freight, Inc. of Warren, Ohio, owned a fleet of trucks and also used lease operators. This 1957 DC-75 Autocar owned by Robert Hagberg, based out of Detroit, is pulling a company-owned Trailmobile trailer. The Cummins-powered black-and-red Autocar sleeper could be seen anywhere in the Daniels territory from east St. Louis, Illinois, to Jersey City, New Jersey. A total of 470 tractors and 544 trailers made up the fleet. *Neil Sherff*

In 1957, Watson Bros. Transportation Co. of Omaha, Nebraska, was considered the sixth-largest trucking company in the United States. This 1957 International DCO Emeryville and Fruehauf reefer trailer is one unit of more than 2,800 in the fleet. These trucks traveled from Chicago to Denver and on to San Francisco, as well as from Denver to Albuquerque, through the Southwest into Los Angeles. The photo was taken in front of the Joslyn Art Museum in Omaha. *Watson Bros. Transportation Co.*

Although Chicago and the eastern half of Wisconsin is not a very large geographic area, a company like Olson Transportation Co. of Green Bay still required a sizable fleet. Olson served its area with 242 tractors and 271 various types of trailers, including this BC International and Trailmobile reefer trailer. *Lefebvre-Luebke Photographers*

A lot of the western trucking companies used conventional long-nose tractors like this Diamond T tractor with a reefer trailer. Denver-Chicago Trucking Co. used four or five different makes of conventional tractors west of Denver. *Denver Chicago Trucking Co.*

Without a sleeper box, a tractor's wheelbase can make it look longer than it really is. The square-fender International and Pike trailer make for a nice unit. Blue and white was the color scheme for Gould Transportation Co. based in Los Angeles. *Gould Transportation Co.*

Household goods carriers typically use owner-operator tractors to pull their trailers. North American Van Lines of Fort Wayne, Indiana, and this owner's Diamond T tractor pull a company-owned Trailmobile trailer. The company colors were maroon and cream with a black stripe. *Harry Patterson*

Texas had a number of refrigerated carriers based throughout the state, including Frozen Food Express, Inc. of Dallas. A total of nine terminals stretched from California to Texas and up to Chicago. The fleet was made up of 90 owner-operator rigs. *Ron Adams collection*

A B-73 Mack and two Highway trailers make up this train somewhere along the New York State Thruway, where double 40-foot trailers were starting to come onto the scene. John Vogel, Inc. of Albany, New York, was one of many companies that had this kind of operation. *John Vogel, Inc.*

Husmann and Roper Freight Lines, Inc. of St. Louis, Missouri, was one of the smaller companies, with four terminals from St. Louis to Cincinnati and a fleet of 75 tractors and 115 trailers. The name Schien probably has a connection with Schien Truck Lines of Sedalia, Missouri. Husmann and Roper became part of Interstate Motor Lines of Salt Lake City in the early 1960s. *Holtsnider Studios*

As the map shows on the side of the trailer, Akron-Chicago Transportation Co. of Akron, Ohio, served five states around the Great Lakes area from Chicago to Utica, New York. The fleet consisted of 140 tractors and 190 trailers, including this B-67 Mack and Ohio Body Co. trailer. Painted on the door of the cab is "E & F Trucking, Inc.," which was probably a small fleet operator leased to Akron-Chicago. *Mel Sutter Studios*

Reece Lines of New Providence, Iowa, was one of the many livestock haulers in the Midwest. This 1958 International DCO Emeryville and Chamberlin trailer was one of the fleet. The picture was probably taken at the Chicago stockyards. *Neil Sherff*

Consolidated Forwarding Co. of St. Louis ran its blue-and-orange fleet of 186 tractors and 293 trailers among 12 terminals from Dallas to Milwaukee and east to Cincinnati. This 1958 International DCO Emeryville and Fruehauf trailer were part of the fleet. *Holtsnider Studios*

Olson Transportation Co. ran this International BC Diesel and Trailmobile converta-flat trailer. The color scheme for Olson was maroon, black, and yellow with a red stripe. *Olson Transportation Co.*

Dromedary rigs were rare in the East in the 1950s. Gilbert Carrier Corp. used them, however, to haul garments from New York City's garment district to California. This International DCO Emeryville with Strick Dromedary body and Strick trailer was among the rigs in the black-and-yellow Gilbert fleet. *Neil Sherff*

Making its way across a big bridge span in 1958 was this CO Model International and Fruehauf trailer. Associated Transport Co. of New York City had a fleet of 1,334 tractors and 2,113 trailers. The equipment was stationed among 46 terminals from Atlanta to Boston and west to Cincinnati. Associated Transport was probably the largest trucking company at this time. *Associated Transport Co.*

Small icicles on the bumper tell us that this picture was taken during the dreaded winter season. Best Way, Inc. of Terre Haute, Indiana, faced the challenge of poor weather and worse road conditions with this 1959 Diamond T and Strick trailer. *WTHI-TV*

The happy man in the cab of this G-75 Mack is probably the owner of the tractor—the company-owned trailer is a Highway. Greyhound Van Lines, Inc. hauled household goods countrywide. *Greyhound Van Lines, Inc.*

Greenstein Trucking Co. of Pompano Beach, Florida, hauled produce throughout the eastern half of the United States. The photo of this G-73 Mack and Great Dane produce trailer were taken around 1959 in the Michigan or Chicago area. The Greenstein colors were, of course, green and white. *Neil Sherff*

Western Truck Lines, Inc. of Los Angeles used Dromedary rigs like this 1959 White-Freightliner tractor and Fruehauf trailer—one unit of the 656 in the fleet. This photo was probably taken at the time when the two carriers, Western Truck Lines and Gillette Motor Transport of Dallas, were merging into one company. *Western-Gillette, Inc.*

There were a number of large trucking companies based in North Carolina, among them Hennis Freight Lines of Winston-Salem, operating this H-67 Mack and Trailmobile trailer as part of its fleet of 225 tractors and 425 trailers in 1959. *Hennis Freight Lines*

Robert H. Carr & Sons, Inc. of Frazer was a long-distance milk hauler from Pennsylvania. This late-1950s A-75 Autocar and Heil milk tank trailer were in the fleet. *Autocar Trucks*

Murphy Transportation Co. of Hampton, Iowa, was one of the larger livestock haulers. This green-and-white GMC "Crackerbox" cab-over and Chamberlin "Possum-belly" livestock trailer represent what the fleet looked like. *Murphy Transportation Co.*

Los Angeles-Seattle Motor Express, Inc. of Seattle ran primarily along the West Coast. It had a variety of makes and types of trucks, among them this late-1950s Peterbilt and Utility reefer trailer. *Los Angeles-Seattle Motor Express, Inc.*

The Great Lakes states had a lot of steel hauler companies, like Brada Cartage Co. of Detroit. This very sharp-looking DC-75 Autocar, with the famous fancy Michigan pinstriping, is pulling a spread-axle flatbed trailer with sides. The name Orland on the grille guard is probably that of the owner. *Neil Sherff*

This 1959 Diamond T sleeper tractor and Dorsey reefer trailer help Ruke haul produce out of Florida. *Neil Sherff*

Whitfield Transportation Co. of El Paso, Texas, owns this late-1950s Peterbilt Dromedary rig and Utility trailer as part of a fleet of 22 tractors and 31 trailers. Six terminals between El Paso and Salt Lake City made up the company operations. *Whitfield Transportation Co.*

A number of Canadian carriers made their way into the United States. One of the smaller was Mexi-Cana Reefer Services, Ltd. of Vancouver, British Columbia. The tractor, a Canadian Hayes, looks like it's unit No. 2 in the fleet. *Brian Williams*

It was a long hard run over the Rocky Mountains. This B-75 Mack tractor and American reefer trailer took it on for Midwest Coast Transport, Inc. of Sioux Falls, South Dakota. The huge Aero-Liner sleeper box gives this Mack the extra tough look. *Midwest Coast Transport, Inc.*

Here we have a B-73 from the Mack family of trucks, for Greenstein Trucking of Pompano Beach, Florida. The fender mirrors, dual air horns, air conditioner, and dual stacks of this Mack B-73 give this tractor a sharp, tough-looking appearance for the produce-hauling line. The trailer is a Fruehauf with a belly-mount reefer unit. *Neil Sherff*

This White 9022 TD was probably the shortest conventional tractor with the smallest cab, designed to pull 40-foot trailers within areas having 50-foot-length laws and to cut down weight for more payload. Roadway Express, Inc. of Akron, Ohio, and many other carriers had lots of these tractors in their fleets. *White Motor Co.*

With a fleet of 175 tractors and 199 trailers, Southwest Freight Lines of Kansas City, Missouri, could provide its customers with the service they expected. Open-tops, reefers, vans, and flatbeds made up the trailer fleet. This 9000 White and Highway van trailer were part of the fleet. *Jay-Bee Photography courtesy Aluminum Company of America*

Safeway Truck Lines of Chicago had been around for about 20 years in 1959. Their primary cargo was refrigerated products from Colorado in the west to Maine in the east. A fleet of 180 tractor-trailer units, almost all owner-operators, did the hauling for Safeway. One of those units was this Diamond T sleeper tractor and Fruehauf trailer. *Neil Sherff*

The 1958 International DCO Emeryville and twin Fruehauf open-top trailers were one of the many sets of double-40s that ran along the Ohio-Indiana Turnpikes, the New York State Thruway, and the Massachusetts Turnpike in 1959. At this time, Motor Cargo, Inc. was becoming part of the Consolidated Freightways operation to make C.F. the second coast-to-coast carrier. *Ron Adams collection*

Lynden Transfer, Inc. of Lynden, Washington, frequently ran north to Alaska as part of its operations. This 1958 Kenworth is decked out with the Alaska running gear (chains, sanders, and frame-mounted fuel tank) pulling an Aero-Liner reefer trailer. Lynden colors were green with a white stripe. *Lynden Transfer, Inc.*

P. Salvino Transport was a very small operation, judging from the numbers on the tractor and trailer. This 1958 Kenworth and Brown trailer make a tasteful-looking combination. Notice the unusual stack setup on the tractor. *Kenworth Truck Co.*

Interstate Motor Lines of Salt Lake City, as it was still named in the 1950s, ran from the Pacific Coast to as far east as St. Louis and Chicago. The colors for I.M.L. were yellow on green. The White-Freightliner tractor and Strick trailer show what the I.M.L. equipment looked like in 1958. *Strick Trailers*

Although the operations have existed since 1929, Ryder Truck Lines did not exist by name until some 30 years later in 1959. The previous name was Great Southern Trucking Co. of Jacksonville, Florida. At that time, Ryder covered a six-state area in the South with a fleet of 377 tractors and 744 trailers. One of those units was this White 9000 tractor and Great Dane van trailer. The company also operated a tank lines division and a rental system. Ryder became part of International Utilities, as did P-I-E, and later Ryder-P-I-E became one. *Ryder Truck Lines, Inc.*

Hauling household goods was always a good, steady business for trucking companies. Whether it was from one side of town to the other or cross-country, people had to be moved. One of the moving companies that was available to do the job was Andrews Van Lines, Inc. of Norfolk, Nebraska. One of the trucks in the fleet was this late-1950s International Emeryville DCO tractor and Fruehauf moving trailer that looks like it was operated by a father-and-son team, Les Jr. and Les Sr. *Andrews Van Lines, Inc.*

Years ago, the rigs in the West were always bigger than those in the East. Pacific Truck Service in San Jose, California, had this B-75 Mack to haul petroleum in the tank body throughout California. *Ron Adams collection*

At first glance this truck looks like a Ford. In fact, it's actually a Mack N Series, made from 1957 to 1962. These cabs were built by the Budd Company but were sold to both Ford and Mack. Consolidated Freight Co. of Saginaw, Michigan, had this one hauling in its steel division. It was one in a fleet of 232 tractors and 412 trailers. In the early 1960s, Consolidated merged with Kramer Bros. Freight Lines, Inc. of Detroit to become known as Kramer-Consolidated Freight Lines, Inc. until Transcon Lines, Inc. bought them out in 1966. *Neil Sherff*

One of the smaller carriers in the later 1950s, Ecklar-Moore Express, Inc. of Cynthiana, Kentucky, offered service to three Midwestern states with a fleet of 55 tractors and 117 trailers. Shown here is one of its C-1000 Fords and a Fruehauf trailer. *Ecklar-Moore Express, Inc.*

Long-wheelbase conventional tractors were common with a lot of the Western carriers, including Ringsby Truck Lines, Inc. of Denver. This orange-and-black Peterbilt tractor pulled a reefer trailer hauling meat and frozen foods west of Denver. *Ringsby Truck Lines, Inc.*

Brady Motorfrate, Inc. of Des Moines, Iowa, and Days Transfer, Inc. of Elkhart, Indiana, eventually merged and became Brady-Days, Inc. with headquarters in Des Moines. This Crackerbox GMC pulling a Strick trailer, and the AC International pulling a Fruehauf trailer, were part of a combined fleet of 577 units that served 10 Midwestern states. *Brady-Days, Inc.*

Sterling Transit, Inc. of Montebello was strictly a California carrier. A 1977 carrier directory states that Sterling had a fleet of 105 tractors and 191 trailers. However, some 18 years earlier, judging from the number on the tractor, it looks like Sterling was just starting in the trucking business. The company had six terminals and offered overnight-every night service. *Utility Trailer Co.*

Back in the 1950s, two-lane highways were common. This late-1950s Kenworth CBE tractor and Utility trailer were part of the Denver-Chicago Trucking Co., Inc. fleet. *Denver-Chicago Trucking Co., Inc.*

Canadian Freightways, Ltd. of Calgary, Alberta, was the Canadian Division of Consolidated Freightways, Inc. of California. This late-1950s White-Freightliner and matching Utility doubles were among 65 tractors and 93 trailers in the Canadian fleet. *Canadian Freightways, Ltd.*

The South had a number of large trucking companies, Mercury Motor Express, Inc. of Birmingham, Alabama, among them. One of the units in the orange-and-black fleet was this Diamond T tractor and van trailer. *Mercury Motor Express, Inc.*

Hauling construction equipment and farm machinery were two of the specialties of International Transport, Inc. of Rochester, Minnesota. Here a DCO International Emeryville and flatbed trailer haul a trench digger and an International bulldozer with Drott bucket. *International Transport, Inc.*

CHAPTER SIX
GOING COAST TO COAST IN THE 1960s

New model development and ongoing consolidation in the trucking industry continued into the 1960s. In 1963, Kenworth went from the narrow radiator to the wide-front hood on its conventional model W-900 and restyled the cab-over-engine model. Kenworth eliminated the skirt from the lower part of the cab behind the front wheel. The stacks were also brace-mounted to the frame instead of the cab. In 1962, Mack introduced its new F series cab-over-engine tractor, and followed in 1964 with the new R series conventional cab design. Mack also reworked the western series tractors, the FL and RL, as well as the MB low cab-over-engine model, while Mack's C series only lasted from 1963 to 1965. In 1955, Autocar introduced the new A series with an aluminum radiator shell. In 1966, Marmon came out with its first cab-over-engine model.

In 1968, White-Freightliner introduced a first in the industry: a 104-inch cab-over known as the Vanliner. That same year Peterbilt introduced its wide-front radiator on the conventional model known as the 359, and also made some styling changes on the cab-over-engine model. White restyled its 9000 model, introducing the new 7000 model cab-over, the White Compact, and the new Western Star series in 1969. International came out with the altogether-new 1965 CO 4000 cab-over and the new 1964 Fleetstar and 1963 Load Star conventional. In 1969, the International Transtar was launched. This provided a more customized cab, which could accommodate bigger engines.

In 1968, GMC and Chevrolet came out with new models: the GMC Astro 95 and the Chevrolet Titan 90. The 9500 series for GMC came in long-hood and short-hood

During the late 1940s and early 1950s, a number of refrigerated haulers got their start in the trucking business. One of those companies was Trans-Cold Express, Inc. of Dallas. Trans-Cold was basically an owner-operator lease company that covered almost all the 48 states. During the mid- to late 1960s, Trans-Cold had one of the sharpest-looking fleets of trucks on the road. This is a long-nose 9000 White tractor with a Utility reefer trailer. Trans-Cold Express, Inc. was owned by Midwest-Emery Freight System of Chicago. *Brian Williams*

The truck-trailer combination was a typical setup in the western states. They came in various types-this one happens to be a rack-side body mounted on an early-1960s Peterbilt truck. J-Ways Trucking Co., Inc. of Silverton, Oregon, used this combination for hauling along the Pacific Coast. *Brian Williams*

versions. Ford brought out the new Louisville series in 1969 along with the new W series high cab-over-engine model. The merger of REO and Diamond T gave us the new Diamond REO line in 1967.

Following on the heels of the creation of the nation's second coast-to-coast carrier-when Consolidated Freightway bought out Motor Cargo, Inc.-other companies joined forces to stay competitive. In 1961, Navajo Freight Lines of Denver took over General Expressway, Inc. of Chicago. In 1962, Watson Bros. Transportation Co. of Omaha, Nebraska, took over Wilson Trucking Corp. of Waynesboro, Virginia. And in 1966, Interstate Motor Lines of Salt Lake City, Utah, bought out Eastern Motor Dispatch (E-M-D) of Columbus, Ohio. Still other acquisitions in 1966 included Transcon Lines of Los Angeles buying out Kramer-Consolidated Freight Lines, Inc. of Detroit. And Pacific Intermountain Express (P-I-E) of Oakland, California, took over All States Freight, Inc. of Akron, Ohio. Time Freight, Inc. of Lubbock, Texas, bought out Super Service Motor Freight, Inc. of Nashville, Tennessee. Then in 1969, Time Freight, Inc., Los Angeles-Seattle Motor Express, and Denver Chicago Trucking Co. merged to form a giant nationwide carrier, TIME-

DC, Inc., with headquarters in Lubbock, Texas.

Other mergers and buyouts occurring during the 1960s included McLean Trucking Co. and Chicago Express, Inc.; Smith Transfer Co. and Brady-Days, Inc.; Mason and Dixon Lines and Yankee Lines; Eastern Express, Inc. and Wheelock Bros.; United Truck Lines and Buckingham Transportation Co.; Lee Way Motor Freight and Texas-Arizona Motor Freight; Adley Express and Miller Motor Express; Wilson Freight Co. and Freightways, Inc. and Interstate Dispatch were included in the Wilson buyout. Branch Motor Express and Middle Atlantic Transportation Co.; ACE Transportation Co. and Great Lakes Express; East Texas Motor Freight and Lee American Freight System; Gordons Transport and Valley Copperstate Sunset Lines; Eazor Express and Daniels Motor Freight; and lastly, United Buckingham and Norwalk Truck Lines, which merged before being taken over by Ringsby Truck Lines to form Ringsby United, Inc.

Through the 1960s, as the interstate highway system became more complete, trucking companies were able to make faster deliveries. Truck stops also improved, offering more services for the increasing number of over-the-road drivers.

Strickland Transportation Co., Inc. of Dallas served the area from Texas to the Great Lakes and on to the East Coast. Strickland got its routes to the East Coast after the purchase of Kelleher Motor Freight Lines, Inc. of St. Louis. One of the units that Strickland used in its system was this early-1960s International Emeryville DCO tractor and Brown trailer. The total fleet consisted of approximately 350 tractors and 500 trailers. *Strickland Transportation Co., Inc.*

Midwest Emery Freight System was the new name after the merger of Emery Transportation Co. and Midwest Freight Co. both of Chicago. Their primary business was "Haulers of Food Stuffs." They also had a tank lines operation. The fleet consisted of both company-owned tractors and lease operators. One of the tractors was this circa 1960 G-75 Mack and Trailmobile reefer trailer. The company colors were black and yellow. *Neil Sherff*

As the lengths of trailers increased, so did the gross weight. As this happened, more of the eastern trucking companies went to tandem-axle tractors. Here we see a B-67 tandem-axle Mack pulling a Strick reefer trailer for Eastern Express, Inc. of Terre Haute, Indiana. Notice that the name was changed from Eastern Motor Express to Eastern Express, Inc. *Eastern Express, Inc.*

This is a good comparison photo of two different trailers. The tractor is a G-75 Mack pulling two of the same type of Fruehauf trailers. Both are stainless steel, but the front one is an early-1960s era and the back one is from the early 1950s. The first one has air suspension while the second has torsion bar suspension. Manufacturers-Lake Shore Motor Freight of Girard, Ohio, owns this set of turnpike doubles. *Manufacturers-Lake Shore, Inc.*

This 1960 White 5400 TD tractor is set to pull the first set of double trailers for Bolin Drive-Away Co. of Cleveland, Ohio. The picture was taken in May 1960 at the Towpath Service Plaza on the Ohio Turnpike. The men in the picture are the Bolin driver and four Bolin officials. *Scope Photographers*

Home Transfer Co. of Portland, Oregon, was a refrigerated carrier hauling throughout the western United States. The long-wheelbase White-Freightliner and Brown reefer trailer show the kind of equipment that Home Transfer ran. Judging from the number on the tractor, Home had a sizable fleet. *Home Transfer Co.*

Willis Shaw Frozen Express of Elm Springs, Arkansas, was another refrigerated carrier. According to Moody's Transportation manual, Willis Shaw started in May of 1958. Shaw had a fleet of both White-Freightliner and Kenworth tractors. This is an early-1960s Kenworth with a Trailmobile reefer trailer. *Ray M. Watson*

Texas, being a big oil state, had several tank lines' carriers based in the state, including Robertson Tank Lines, Inc. of Houston. One of the trucks in the fleet was this circa 1960 International DCO Emeryville tractor and 7,025-gallon-capacity Butler tank trailer. *Ron Adams collection*

Frozen Food Express, Inc. of Dallas hauled frozen foods and other products requiring refrigeration. The main operating area at this time was from California through the Southwest, into Texas and up through the central part of the country. The fleet was mainly made up of lease operator rigs such as this early-1960s Kenworth and Fruehauf reefer trailer. *Neil Sherff*

In 1960, two of these Hendrickson tractors were made for pulling turnpike doubles for Cooper Jarrett Motor Freight Lines of Chicago. They had big powerful Detroit diesels in them. Cooper Jarrett was always known as the "Route of the Relay" carrier. *Detroit Diesel*

Trucks like this were known as "Michigan Centipedes," because of the 13 axles. George Alger & Co. of Detroit was a steel products hauling company, and had several of these in the fleet. The Alger colors were black and orange, which made this Hendrickson look rather impressive. *Neil Sherff*

Pirkle Refrigerated Freight Lines of Cudahy, Wisconsin, was an almost all owner-operator fleet. One of the trucks in the fleet was this 920 Diamond T and Fruehauf trailer that was driven by Hamilton Lord in 1962-63. The Pirkle Trucks loaded in Illinois and Wisconsin for California, which was a four- to five-day trip. *Neil Sherff*

Specialized carriers haul different loads on almost every trip. At Progressive Transportation Co. of Compton, California, the crew with this circa 1960 Peterbilt probably considered this load as just another day's work. The 13-axle setup was needed to haul the long cumbersome load to its destination. *Progressive Transportation Co.*

Wales Trucking Co. of Grand Prairie, Texas, was a 48-state carrier hauling various specified products. The owner of this B-61 Mack equipped his tractor with an aluminum sleeper box for the long runs. *Neil Sherff*

Operating out of Florida and Georgia, Watkins Motor Lines of Thomasville, Georgia, hauled a lot of produce and frozen food loads up into Illinois and Michigan. One of Watkins' trucks was this B-61 Mack sleeper and Fruehauf reefer trailer. *Neil Sherff*

One of the companies that got its start during the Depression was Cooper Jarrett Motor Freight Lines of Chicago. Operating 10 terminals between Boston and Kansas City, Missouri, gave it a wide operating territory. The GMC tractor and Trailmobile trailer were part of a 480-unit fleet. *Cooper Jarrett, Inc.*

From north of the border, we have this A-10264 Autocar powered by a 250-horsepower Cummins diesel pulling a Fruehauf cattle trailer. Lupul Transport, Ltd. of Edmonton, Alberta, was the owner of the rig. *Autocar Trucks*

Being an over-the-road truck driver provides the opportunity to see many places and lots of beautiful scenery. Drivers for Canadian Freightways, Ltd. of Calgary, Alberta, would have seen valleys, prairies, plains, and the beautiful Canadian Rockies along their routes. This White-Freightliner tractor with an Aero-Liner refrigerated Dromedary body and an Aero-Liner trailer are parked in front of the scenic Canadian Rockies. Units like this were common in this Canadian fleet. *Canadian Freightways, Ltd.*

On this Canadian Freightways White-Freightliner tractor is a removable Dromedary body that looks like it could be a Fruehauf. The trailer is a reefer and looks like it could also be a mid- to late-1950s Fruehauf. *Canadian Freightways, Ltd.*

Another livestock hauler was Peters Bros., Inc. of Lenhartsville, Pennsylvania. The 1960 Kenworth tractor and Wilson livestock trailer made three trips one week and two trips the following week from Allentown to Chicago and back hauling hogs. The tractor was painted two-tone green with a red frame and had a 335-horsepower Cummins diesel. The proud driver of this rig was Warren Phillips. This was one of the first Kenworths in Pennsylvania. *Neil Sherff*

This photograph can be deceiving. It looks like the tractor is extra large, but in fact it's the smaller-than-usual trailer that makes it look that way. Edward M. Rude Carrier Corp. of Falling Waters, West Virginia, had a fleet of these 220 Cummins-powered DC75T Autocar tractors. The small trailers were used for hauling explosives. The few added extras, such as dual stacks, dual air horns, fender mirrors, and chrome luberfiner, on these tractors really made them stand out above the rest. *Autocar Trucks*

As we can see, there are eight cars on this truck. Given today's smaller cars, this truck would be able to haul anywhere from 11 to 13 cars now. This GMC auto hauler was owned by the Pacific Motor Trucking Co. of San Francisco. This is the western-type car hauler—carriers in the East used four-car haulers. *Pacific Motor Trucking Co.*

"Humpin' to Please" was the slogan on the trucks for Campbell "66" Express of Springfield, Missouri, as they traveled through their operating territory and on the famous Route 66. The Diamond T tractor and Fruehauf reefer trailer are typical of the equipment they had. *Campbell "66" Express*

Another company that used turnpike doubles was Spector Freight System of Chicago. This White 9000 and Twin Fruehaufs pretty well speaks for the rest of the fleet. Notice that the sign on the side of each trailer still shows Spector-Mid States. *Spector Freight System*

In order to cover 11 western states, Garrett Freightlines of Pocatello, Idaho, had a variety of vehicles to serve its customers. This is an early-1960s Kenworth tractor and a Pike trailer. *Garrett Freightlines*

Texas Meat Packers in Dallas was known as the largest independent meat packer in the Southwest. This White-Freightliner tractor and Wilson livestock trailer hauled the cattle from range to packing house. The photo was taken at the Wilson plant in Sioux City, Iowa. *Woodworth Commercial Photos*

There were many steel haulers in Ohio. The big F-1000 Ford truck-trailer combination is a typical Ohio-type steel rig owned by Detroit-Pittsburgh Motor Freight, Inc. of Cleveland. *Detroit-Pittsburgh Motor Freight*

Some companies had a few divisions other than general freight. Jones Truck Lines of Springdale, Arkansas, had a reefer division called the Eskimotive Division, covering from Alabama and Texas in the South to Colorado in the West and Illinois and Indiana in the North. The International DCO Emeryville and American reefer trailer make a cool trip together. *Jones Truck Lines*

Two for the Price of One—this doubles set ran the New York State Thruway for Oneida Motor Freight, Inc. of Oneida, New York. The B-61 Mack and two Strick trailers were the team on this trip. *Oneida Motor Freight, Inc.*

From the Grand Canyon country of Pennsylvania is a company that got its start in 1947. H. W. Taynton Co. from Wellsboro, Pennsylvania, had a fleet of 80 tractors and 137 trailers. This 258 Brockway was one of the tractors in the fleet, which served 12 eastern and midwestern states. *H. W. Taynton Co.*

Wilson livestock trailers seemed to be popular among the livestock haulers. L. W. Westhoff of New Vienna, Iowa, matched a Wilson with his International DCO Emeryville to haul livestock in the midwestern states in 1962. *Wilson Trailer Co.*

This GMC tractor and Brown reefer trailer is from 1962. Midwest Emery Freight was one of the biggest reefer haulers out of Chicago, taking them from as far west as Colorado and east into New England. *GMC Truck & Coach*

Eastern car haulers usually only carried four cars until the 1960s, when a fifth had been added. This 1961 Chevrolet tractor for Janesville Auto Transport of Janesville, Wisconsin, is also hauling Chevrolet cars. In 1979, the company had 415 tractors and 401 trailers. When every rig was loaded, they could haul a total of 2,000 cars. *Janesville Auto Transport*

Lambeau Field, the Packers stadium in Green Bay, Wisconsin, was chosen for the background scenery for Olson Transportation Co., owner of this 1962 GMC Dromedary tractor and trailer. The map on the side of the Dromedary body shows the territory Olson covered. Notice the chrome stack, which was rather unusual for a company-owned truck. *Olson Transportation Co.*

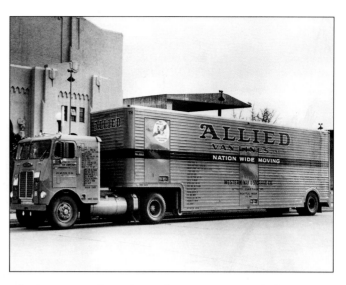

Allied Van Lines of Broadview, Illinois, was among the biggest household goods carriers, with agents all over the United States and Canada. Western Van and Storage Co. was the agent in the Seattle area. The circa 1962 White-Freightliner tractor and Brown moving van trailer helped to do the hauling. *Western Van and Storage Co.*

Companies usually tried to stay with one or two makes of trucks in their fleets. Dohrn Transfer Co. of Rock Island, Illinois, got its start in 1924. This Diamond T tractor and Trailmobile trailer was one of the units in Dohrn's growing fleet. By the 1960s, Dohrn had merged with Chicago-Dubuque Motor Transportation Co. *Dohrn Transfer Co.*

This 1962 International DCO Emeryville tractor and Fruehauf trailer added to the variety of equipment in the Dohrn Transfer Co. fleet. Dohrn covered a five- or six-state area when this photo was taken. *Dohrn Transfer Co.*

What started out as Admiral Transit grew into Admiral-Merchants Cole/Dixie. Admiral Transit purchased Merchants Freight System and became Admiral-Merchants, Inc. Jack Cole Co. and Dixie Highway Express were purchased to make the name Admiral-Merchants/Cole/Dixie. After the purchase of these companies, the fleet totaled 159 tractors and 562 trailers and covered almost the entire eastern half of the United States. In the early 1960s, this 5000 White and Fruehauf trailer were part of the fleet. *Admiral-Merchants, Inc.*

This early-1960s Canadian Kenworth truck with an Aero-Liner reefer body still had the butterfly hood. This is one of four straight trucks in the over-the-road fleet. The other Canadian Freightways over-the-road rigs included approximately 70 tractors and 100 trailers. Canadian Freightways, Ltd. was owned by Consolidated Freightways, Inc. of Menlo Park, California. *Canadian Freightways, Ltd.*

This 1961 White 9000 and Trailmobile trailer likely made many trips on Route 66, which also gave Campbell "66" Express of Springfield, Missouri, its name. *White Motor Co.*

The little bit of snow in this photo was not enough to stop the delivery of this load. International Transport, Inc. of Rochester, Minnesota, kept moving to make deliveries on time. With a mixed fleet of equipment, this owner-operator leased his Cat-powered 1961 International DCO Emeryville and pulled a company trailer. Notice all the license plates that were required for continental traveling at the time. *International Transport, Inc.*

Another company that had a mixed bag of equipment was Navajo Freight Lines of Denver. It seemed as if most of its tractors were Internationals, such as this DCO Emeryville. Fruehauf trailers were also a big part of the fleet. Navajo became the third coast-to-coast carrier when it merged with General Expressways of Chicago in 1961. *Neil Sherff*

East Texas Motor Freight Lines of Dallas ran from Texas and Louisiana up into Illinois. Its fleet at this time consisted of White 9000 tractors and mixed brands of trailers, such as this Lufkin. In its later years, the East Texas fleet totaled 1,509 tractors and 3,640 trailers covering 40 states from coast to coast. *East Texas Motor Freight Lines-ETMF*

A.R. Gundry, Inc. operation hauled petroleum products in six eastern states. This Ford F-1000 had a 534 V-8 engine with a Fuller R-46 transmission. The 35-foot trailer is a Pennsylvania brand. *Ford-Houston Branch*

The OK Trucking Co. of Cincinnati, did O.K. operating in the Midwest. In 1977, its fleet included 346 tractors and more than 900 trailers with 23 terminals in seven states. This B-61 Mack and Fruehauf trailer were part of the OK fleet in 1962. *OK Trucking Co.*

It's been said that some drivers would rather haul explosives than cattle. While explosives will stay in place unless a fatal mistake is made, cattle can shift a lot easier from side to side, causing the driver to lose control of his rig. But the driver of this White-Freightliner truck-trailer cattle rig didn't seem to mind. He hauled for Portland Motor Transport, who was leasing to Jones Truck Line of Baker, Oregon. He also traveled in the comfort of an air-conditioned cab. *Freightliner Corp.*

Double trailers were always a popular combination in the West. Garrett Freightlines was one of the many companies that used them. The Garrett colors of yellow and green were worn proudly on this circa 1962 Kenworth, which is pulling two identical Fruehauf trailers. *Garrett Freightlines*

In the 1960s, a number of farm co-ops were formed, including the Agricultural Transportation Association of Texas Marketing Co-Op of Fort Worth, known as the ATA of Texas. This 1962 Kenworth cab-over-engine tractor and Hobbs reefer trailer was one of the rigs in the fleet, and a very sharp-looking outfit. Notice the stack arrangement, which is unusual for a cab-over tractor. Almost all farm co-ops hauled nationwide. *Don Lloyd Photo*

Lou's Transport, Ltd. of Toronto, Ontario, was hauling bulk cement for the Canada Cement Co. using a 1962 White 4400 TD tractor and a Butler cement tank trailer. *Ross Jamieson*

All kinds of commodities were hauled by truck. Jensen Transport, Inc. of Independence, Iowa, hauled milk as a liquid commodity in the milk tank trailer shown with this early-1960s CT-850 Ford cab-over-engine tractor. It had a 534 SD V-8 engine on a 135-inch wheelbase. The truck ran from Waterloo, Iowa, to St. Louis, Missouri, hauling 5,700 gallons of milk in the 40-foot trailer. *Ford-Houston Branch*

Kroblin Refrigerated X-Press of Sumner, Iowa, was a popular refrigerated carrier from the Midwest. Kroblin ran to the East Coast, hauling produce and frozen foods and using an HT-950-D Ford cab-over-engine tractor and Fruehauf reefer trailer. Kroblin's colors were red and white. *Ford-Houston Branch*

This HF 950-D Ford tractor with a flatbed trailer was owned by Barnes Truck Lines, Inc. of Wilson, North Carolina. The tractor is powered by a Cummins NH-250 on a 158-inch wheelbase with a Fuller R-96 10-speed transmission. Barnes hauled lumber and building products in the eastern half of the United States. *Ford-Houston Branch*

"Ship the Big A" was the slogan for Allegheny Freight Lines, Inc. of Winchester, Virginia. Running over the mountains between Winchester and Pittsburgh, Allegheny felt that a fleet of Fords, such as this Ford H-1000-D, was qualified to do the job. The tractor, powered by an NH-220 Cummins Diesel with an R-96 ten-speed transmission on a 134-inch wheelbase, pulled a 40-foot Trailmobile trailer. *Ford-Houston Branch*

"The Haul of Fame" was a slogan used by Eagle Motor Lines of Birmingham, Alabama, a heavy specialized carrier. By 1977, Eagle had 19 terminals scattered across the United States, with a fleet of 589 tractors and 880 trailers. In 1962, this H-67 Mack tractor was pulling an Alabama flatbed trailer with a load of cast pipes and fittings. *Ken Ives Studio*

Having fancy trucks in refrigerated fleets was very popular in the early 1960s. Midwest Coast Transport, Inc. of Sioux Falls, South Dakota was a carrier that had many of them. Although there was a variety in colors, the basic color scheme was black and green with a white stripe. Add dual chrome stacks, and this circa 1962 White-Freightliner tractor was a sharp-looking rig. The trailer is believed to be a highway reefer. *Neil Sherff*

Today in the eastern United States, auto-hauling rigs like this can be seen. However, in the western states, they were common in the early 1960s. Insured Transporters, Inc. of San Leandro, California, had a number of these. Here we see eight Chevrolet trucks being hauled by a GMC Crackerbox tractor. *Insured Transporters, Inc.*

Many of the pioneer trucking companies that got their start back in the 1930s have long since gone by the wayside. One of those pioneer carriers that has made it and is still in business today is Overnite Transportation Co. of Richmond, Virginia. In 1991, Overnite had a fleet of 5,242 tractors and 12,638 trailers covering almost all the United States. Back in 1962, this F-600 Mack and Strick 40-foot trailer display the type of equipment they had at that time. *Dementi-Foster Photographers*

Another company that planted its roots into trucking in 1934 was Knox Motor Service of Rockford, Illinois, covering Illinois, Iowa, and Wisconsin. The Cat-powered International DCO Emeryville and Fruehauf converta-flat trailer were the type of equipment used in 1962. *Knox Motor Service*

No surprise that this big truck is from Texas. This circa 1962 International 220 Diesel and Loadcraft trailer and dolly are ready to work for Trans Western Transport of Odessa. Its job was probably to haul some kind of heavy machinery or oil field rigging equipment. The tractor is equipped with a winch and chains for loading and tying down the load. *Trans-Western Transport*

In 1977, some 43 years after its founding in 1934, Wilson Freight Co. of Cincinnati had built a system of 65 freight terminals, with another 19 in its steel division. A fleet of 1,033 tractors and 2,151 trailers hauled freight from Maine to Georgia and west to Kansas and Oklahoma. This B-67 Mack tractor and Gindy trailer were part of the family in 1962. *Wilson Freight Co.*

Many companies had other divisions in addition to their regular freight divisions. Consolidated Freightways had about a half-dozen divisions, including a tanker division. This circa 1962 White-Freightliner truck-trailer tanker unit is for hauling gasoline. Given the dry pavement, it looks like the driver is removing his chains. *Consolidated Freightways*

In its earlier years, C. R. England & Sons of Salt Lake City, Utah, had almost all Kenworths in its fleet. It did, however, have at least one 1962 International DCO Emeryville. England hauled a lot of produce out of California to the East Coast in reefer trailers such as this Trailmobile. *Robert J. Parrish*

Rogers Cartage Co. of Oak Lawn, Illinois, got its start in the tanker business in 1934. Today the fleet consists of 101 company-owned tractors, 121 leased tractors, and 385 tank trailers of various types. The company hauls liquid petroleum, acid, and chemicals. This is a GMC Crackerbox pulling a Heil tank trailer around 1962. *Rogers Cartage Co.*

This Rogers GMC Crackerbox is pulling a Butler tank trailer. *Rogers Cartage Co.*

This Rogers-owned Trailmobile tank trailer was used for hauling acid behind another GMC Crackerbox. *Rogers Cartage Co.*

This GMC tractor is the conventional type, pulling a Fruehauf tank trailer used for hauling petroleum for Rogers Cartage. *Rogers Cartage Co.*

The green-and-white trucks for California-based Reliable Transportation Co. were often seen pulling tanker trailers along California highways. This circa 1962 Kenworth is pulling a tank trailer in the Cryogenic Division. *Reliable Transportation Co.*

Southern Tank Lines, Inc. of Louisville, Kentucky, used one of its GMC Crackerbox tractors to pull a Fruehauf tank trailer filled with non-flammable liquids. The slogan for this company was "Lifeline for Liquids." *Southern Tank Lines, Inc.*

Covering a big area from the Gulf States to the Great Lakes was no problem for Gordon's Transport, Inc. of Memphis, Tennessee. It had a fleet of approximately 300 tractors and 1,000 trailers to do the job. One of the tractors was this White 7464 TD and Trailmobile van trailer. The company also had open-top and reefer trailers. *White Motor Co.*

Hermann Forwarding Co. was based in North Brunswick, New Jersey, and was a general freight hauler that got its start in 1933. Some 30 years later, one of the trucks in the fleet is this International Fleetstar 2000 tractor and Strick trailer. The first year that International introduced its new Fleetstar Series was 1963. *Hermann Forwarding Co.*

Coastal Transport Co., Inc. of Houston, Texas, was a liquid bulk carrier for the Southwest. This 1963 GMC 1000 Series tractor pulls a tank trailer used to haul compressed gas. *Coastal Transport Co., Inc.*

Gateway Transportation Co. of La Crosse, Wisconsin, was one of the oldest carriers in the business, having gotten its start way back in 1896. This 1963-era Ford "N-1000" Series tractor is pulling a set of double trailers. Gateway closed the gates in 1979 when it was sold to Maislin Bros. in Canada. *Gateway Transportation Co.*

Tri-State Motor Transit Co. of Joplin, Missouri, was a 48-state carrier hauling many different kinds of cargo related to heavy hauling. The fleet today totals more than 900 tractors and 1,800 trailers. One type of rig used in the fleet in 1963 was this White-Freightliner truck with Aero-Liner body and pull-trailer. The hauler probably used this truck in its western area only. The Tri-State colors are turquoise and white. *Freightliner Corp.*

Another carrier from the Bluegrass state was Killion Motor Express, Inc. of Louisville. The green-and-yellow graphics were seen in a four-state area around Kentucky. One of the trucks on the Louisville-to-Knoxville (Tennessee) run was this HT-950-D Ford and Trailmobile trailer. *Ford-Houston Branch*

Among the carriers serving the eastern seaboard was Northeastern Trucking Co. of Charlotte, North Carolina. Its fleet was mainly Internationals such as this DCO Emeryville and Strick trailer. *Northeastern Trucking Co.*

Roadway has almost become a household name. Roadway Express, Inc. of Akron, Ohio, wanted to make sure no one missed the name painted on the sides of its trailers. Since 1931, the two Rouch Brothers have built Roadway into a transportation giant. Their orange and blue trucks, such as this 1964 HD-950 Ford and Gindy trailer, were seen everywhere in the eastern half of the United States. *Ford-Houston Branch*

Trailers with sliding tandems came into the picture in the 1950s. This trailer tandem is being positioned for weight distribution. Like many carriers, Point Express, Inc. of Charleston, West Virginia, had trailers with sliding tandems such as this 40-foot Trailmobile, which is being pulled by a Ford N-1000-D tractor. Point's operating territory included Ohio, Kentucky, Virginia, and West Virginia. *Ford-Houston Branch*

From the land of the Southwest comes Texas-Oklahoma Express, Inc. of Dallas. A network of 14 terminals covered a four-state area from Texas to Missouri. The 820-unit fleet included this 1963 Ford H-950 and Hobbs reefer trailer. *Texas-Oklahoma Express, Inc.*

One of the biggest companies based in the South was Hennis Freight Lines of Winston-Salem, North Carolina. This 1963 vintage F-600 Mack and Trailmobile trailer is an example of what the Hennis fleet was like at that time. *Hennis Freight Lines*

RUAN Transport, Inc. of Des Moines, Iowa, was founded during the Depression in 1933. RUAN was a tank lines company that by 1985 had 36 terminals to serve the continental states. RUAN was a big user of International trucks, such as this 1963 DF-405, pulling the Fruehauf petroleum tank trailer. *RUAN Transport Corp.*

Schwerman Trucking Co. of Milwaukee, Wisconsin, which got its start in 1913, could be the oldest tank lines carrier in the country, and it's still going strong today. In 1963, this White 9000 was one of the fleet. The colors were black with a red stripe. Today the trucks are white.
Schwerman Trucking Co.

A number of refrigerated and produce carriers were based in Florida, including Florida Refrigerated Service of Dade City, serving the eastern United States and into Canada. One of its units was this International DCO Emeryville and Trailmobile reefer trailer. This driver had a few extra luxuries, with the air conditioning and an extra set of rear-view mirrors. *Chafins Photography*

"Don't Mark It Rush—Just Tag It Baggett" was the slogan for Baggett Transportation Co. of Birmingham, Alabama. The company hauled a lot of explosives and blasting powder in 43 states in 1977 with a fleet of 450 tractors and 1,200 trailers. This Diamond T and Fruehauf bulk storage trailer was one of the fleet in 1964. *Joe Winters Photography*

LaVon Johnson of Bryon, Ohio, thought it to be a good idea to lease his DCO International Emeryville to Wenham Transportation Co. of Cleveland. This made his tractor one of 431 and the Ohio trailer one of 567 in Wenham's fleet. Wenham covered an eight-state area with 17 terminals. *Wenham Transportation Co.*

Texas-Arizona Motor Freight, Inc. of El Paso ran the roadrunner route from California to Texas, where its sand-colored trucks, such as this Kenworth tractor pulling a set of Utility double trailers, could be seen. *Kent Gillman*

Fleet Motor Lines, Inc. of Buffalo, New York, was one of a lot of companies that ran double 40-foot trailers over the New York State Thruway. Here we see a circa 1964 Brockway tractor pulling two Strick trailers. Notice the unusual stack arrangement. *Ron Adams collection*

Yankee Lines, known as the "Route of the Minutemen Company," was one of many companies based in Akron, Ohio. The Brockway tractor and Trailmobile trailer was one of the fleet. *Brockway Trucks*

Baltimore Transfer Co. merged with Motor Freight Express of York, Pennsylvania, to form a fleet of more than 1,100 units in 1964. This International Fleetstar 2000 and Gindy trailer were two of its units. *Motor Freight Express*

The Southern Pacific Railroad, like other railroads, had a trucking division. Pacific Motor Trucking Co. and Southern Pacific Truck Service, shown here, were located in Burlingame, California. Trucks and trailers of different types made up a fleet of more than 7,670 units covering an area from Illinois and Indiana to the Southwest and up the Pacific coast to Washington and Oregon. One such unit was this 1964 International DCO Emeryville and a set of Lufkin doubles. *Lufkin Trailers*

The orange-and-black tractors of Yellow Transit Freight Lines of Kansas City, Missouri, such as this 1964 HD-950 Ford, were a familiar sight on the Midwestern highways. *Yellow Transit Freight Lines*

All States Freight, Inc. of Akron, Ohio, operated from Illinois to Massachusetts. It leased owner-operator rigs like this 1964 Kenworth W-900 and Fruehauf trailer. This model sported a lot of chrome extras with a green paint job and white-and-gold striping. Around this time, All States Freight became part of Pacific Intermountain Express Co., making P-I-E a giant coast-to-coast carrier. *Neil Sherff*

A.C.E. Freight, Inc. of Akron, Ohio, was the new company formed by the merger of A.C.E. Transportation Co. and Freight, Inc. The company operated from Iowa to Massachusetts with a combined fleet of 222 tractors and 278 trailers. The rig pictured here is a mid-1960s White 7000, pulling an Ohio trailer. *A.C.E.-Freight, Inc.*

Branch Motor Express, Inc. of Brooklyn, New York, was a carrier in the Northeast. But over the years it acquired a few companies, and Branch grew into a bigger operation. Three of the several companies that were purchased were Motor Freight Corp., Middle Atlantic Transportation Co., and Great Lakes Express. By 1981, the fleet totaled more than 4,200 units. In the mid 1960s, this big H950 Ford tractor and Strick trailer were part of the fleet. *Branch Motor Express, Inc.*

Pilot Freight Carriers Corp. of Winston-Salem, North Carolina, was founded in 1941. By 1955—in just 14 years—Pilot grew into one of the larger truck lines with terminals along the East Coast from Atlanta, Georgia, to Buffalo and Syracuse, New York. At that time, there were 263 tractors and 343 trailers. The unit shown here is a mid-1960s Diamond T tractor with a Strick trailer. Pilot had quite a number of Diamond Ts in its fleet. *Diamond T Motor Truck Co.*

Despite the Depression, many trucking companies were started in 1931, including Indianhead Truck Lines, Inc. of St. Paul, Minnesota, a nationwide tank lines carrier of petroleum, chemicals, fertilizer, cement, dry bulk materials, and gases. One of the units used to pull tank trailers was this International DF-405 of the mid 1960s. The striking colors made you take a second look. *Indianhead Truck Lines, Inc.*

A lot of trucking companies did not start immediately with trucks. In 1903, even though motor trucks were rapidly appearing on the scene, horse-and-wagon teams were still being used. This is how Brady Motorfrate, Inc. of Des Moines, Iowa, got its start. As the company grew, it acquired several other companies, including Schriebers Trucking Co. of Pittsburgh, Pennsylvania, Days Transfer Co. of Elkhart, Indiana, and Burgmeyer Bros., Inc. of Newark, New Jersey. The company was later purchased by Smith Transfer Corp., of Staunton, Virginia. This 7000 White tractor and Fruehauf reefer trailer show what the Brady equipment was like in the 1960s. *Brady Motorfrate, Inc.*

Some trucking companies used logos to help build their identity. One of the more famous logos was the blue-eyed Indian for Navajo Freight Lines, Inc. of Denver, Colorado. The Navajo trucks featured the Indian wherever they went over the Navajo trails. In 1966, Navajo purchased its first International CO 4000 tractors, to go with Fruehauf trailers such as this. Navajo used a lot of International tractors over the years. *Donne's Studio*

Since 1913, Rollo Trucking Corp., Inc. of Keyport, New Jersey, has been in the tanker hauling business, transporting petroleum acids, chemicals, inedible oils, and other liquids. Some 50 years later, this 1964 B-61 Mack tractor and Heil tank trailer was one of the rigs in the Rollo fleet. *Rollo Trucking Corp., Inc.*

In 1932, Interstate Motor Freight System of Grand Rapids, Michigan, had 8 terminals and 148 units. Ten years later, the totals were 89 terminals and 2,900 units. By 1964, Interstate made its way as far west as Denver. This Cat-powered Dodge 1000 pulled a 40-foot Highway open-top trailer in 1964. *Dodge Trucks*

These red-and-yellow trucks belonging to Michigan Express, Inc. (MX) of Sterling Heights, Michigan, were a familiar sight on the nation's highways. MX had a variety of makes of trucks and trailers, scattered among 45 terminals in 6 states. One of those units was this Ford HD-1000 and Strick trailer. MX's irregular route authority was to haul new furniture from Michigan through the 48 states. *Michigan Express, Inc.*

Hauling Michigan-style requires a lot of axles. This type of rig, known as a Michigan Centipede, had 12 axles and a total of 46 tires. Hayes Sand & Gravel Co. in Livonia, Michigan, made full use of every axle, and hauled the massive trailer with this F-700 Mack. *Neil Sherff*

Another rig in the Michigan Centipede fleet was this International DCO Emeryville with matching Fruehauf trailers. Pinstriping was a Michigan feature. *Neil Sherff*

Akers Motor Lines of Gastonia, North Carolina, had 39 terminals stretching from Georgia to Massachusetts and a fleet of 698 tractors and 1,289 trailers. This F-600 Mack and Strick reefer pose nicely for a quick picture. *Akers Motor Lines*

From the Gulf to the Great Lakes, Viking Freight Co. of St. Louis, Missouri, served the central part of the country with 19 terminals. The White-Freightliner tractor and Trailmobile trailer were kept busy doing what tractor-trailers do best. *Viking Freight Co.*

Eastern Express, Inc. of Terre Haute, Indiana, expanded its operations in the 1960s by taking over Wheelock Bros., Inc. This took Eastern as far west as Denver. The 9000 White tractor and Fruehauf trailer were typical Eastern equipment in 1964. *Eastern Express, Inc.*

Deaton Truck Lines, Inc. of Birmingham, Alabama, operated in the Gulf Coast states from Florida to Louisiana. In 1981, the fleet included 400 tractors and 800 trailers. This White 7000 pulled a Trailmobile trailer in 1964. *Graphic Photo Service*

Chicago-Kansas City Freight Lines, Inc. of Kansas City, Missouri, was a smaller carrier serving the stops between its namesake cities. A smaller company, it had 90 tractors and 350 trailers in 1981. This White-Freightliner and Strick trailer are from 1964. *Chicago-Kansas City Freight Lines*

Founded in 1926, Ogden and Moffett, Inc. of Marysville, Michigan, was a pioneer trucking company in the Great Lakes region. In 1978, it bought out Hooker Motor Freight, Inc. of Grand Rapids, Michigan. Its fleet consisted of 128 tractors and 467 trailers. This 1964-era Dodge tractor pulled a Fruehauf spread-axle trailer. *Port Huron Times Herald*

Like many other moving companies, Pan American Van Lines of Melrose, New York, covered all 48 contiguous states. It got its start in 1956. This GMC 4000 Series is equipped with a Matlock & Cope truck body painted in the company's signature blue-and-white colors. *Pan American Van Lines*

Jack Cole Co. of Birmingham, Alabama, served 10 states in the South, Midwest, and Northeast. This 1964-era GMC and Fruehauf trailer are typical of the trucks that were in the fleet at this time. Years later, Cole became part of Admiral-Merchants, Cole/Dixie. *Graphic Photo Service*

Coastal Tank Lines, Inc. moved to Akron, Ohio, from York, Pennsylvania. Starting with one terminal in 1934, the company expanded to 24 terminals in its 50-year history. In 1964, this White 7000 and Heil petroleum tank trailer carried liquid and dry bulk commodities in 48 states. *Henry M. Blatner*

Truck-trailer combinations were designed to haul the maximum payload possible while remaining within the legal length limits. Fairchild General Freight, Inc. of Yakima, Washington, hauled in six western states and into Canadian provinces. This 1964 White-Freightliner with Aero-liner truck body and pull-trailer stretched out a full 65 feet. Both truck and trailer were equipped with rollers in the floors. *Fairchild General Freight, Inc.*

Holloway Motor Express, Inc. of Gadsden, Alabama, took some time out to get one of its trucks ready for a photo shoot. The 1964 International DCO Emeryville and Great Dane trailer was one in the fleet that hauled from Alabama and Georgia to Tennessee, Missouri, and Kansas. *Holloway Motor Express, Inc.*

The bright yellow trucks of Thunderbird Freight Lines, Inc. of Phoenix could be found throughout southern California, southern Arizona, and southern New Mexico. This 131 Kenworth tractor and twin 297 Fruehauf freight-and-livestock combination trailers plied the route between Los Angeles and Albuquerque. *10 West Studios*

International Transport, Inc. of Rochester, Minnesota, left little room for anything else but these John Deere farm tractors set to roll behind a Kenworth K-100 truck tractor. This company hauled steel products and machinery throughout the 48 states and Canada. In 1977, it had 910 tractors and 1,500 trailers spread among 19 terminals. *International Transport, Inc.*

Having different types of trucks and trailers in a fleet helps a company meet a variety of customer needs. Fairchild General Freight, Inc. of Yakima, Washington, had a versatile fleet, including this truck-trailer combination. The White-Freightliner truck with a Utility body and Utility pull trailer were probably contracted to Owens-Illinois Corp. to haul glass products. Both the body and trailer are the high-cube type. *Brian Williams*

Loading personal household goods for the American families who were on the move was a very delicate operation. Lots of care had to be used in the loading and stacking of these personal goods. U.S. Van Lines, Inc. did just that and boasted that "Your Best Move Is U.S." The personal goods traveled in style in this K100 Kenworth tractor and Fruehauf furniture van trailer. *U.S. Van Lines, Inc.*

Double trailers weren't seen in the eastern states until deregulation 1983. In the West and in Canada, they were common, although not many were used with moving companies. Mackie's Van & Storage, Ltd., Canadian agents for North American Van Lines, did use doubles in its operation. The K100 Kenworth tractor and Trailmobile furniture trailers got the job done on another "Mackie Move." *Croton Studios, Ltd.*

In 1964, Mack introduced the new western series, the RL 700 conventional and the FL 700 cab-over-engine, both made in its new Hayward, California, plant. One of the trucking companies interested in this new cab-over series was Navajo Freight Lines, Inc. of Denver. This lineup of nine brand-new FL 700 Macks waits for the final touch-up of license plates before they start serving their tour of duty over the road. *LeDonne's Studio*

Almost every trucking company had two fleets of trucks, an over-the-road fleet and a city delivery fleet. Eazor Express, Inc. of Pittsburgh, Pennsylvania, was no exception. The city fleet never outnumbered the over-the-road fleet, but the large trucking companies had city fleets large enough to make a nice-size trucking company of their own. Lighter and smaller tractors were used for this purpose, like this Dodge 800 Series. *Eazor Express, Inc.*

Willig Freight Lines, Inc. of San Francisco began in 1923 and grew steadily over the years. In 1955, Willig had a fleet of 50 tractors and 98 trailers. By 1981, the fleet grew to 138 tractors and 227 trailers, and in 1990, 528 tractors and 1,140 trailers served the state of California through eight terminals. One of those units was this White-Freightliner tractor and Brown double trailers. This outfit looks really nice posed in front of the St. Ignatius Church at the University of San Francisco. *Willig Freight Lines, Inc.*

This 1964 REO tractor was owned by Jim Gross of Grand Rapids, Michigan. He leased his rig to the steel division of Great Lakes Express, Inc. in Saginaw. This fine-looking piece of equipment sits proudly, waving the flag for number 9414 among all that Michigan-style pinstriping. A few years later, the name would read Diamond REO. *Neil Sherff*

The round discs that made up part of this load were too wide for the trailer, so the side panels had to be removed to accommodate the extra width. National Transport 101 of Bridgeport, Connecticut, was the carrier and owner of the B-67 Mack and the Strick converta-flat trailer. *National Transport 101*

Can you guess how many pieces of lumber are on this load? There are approximately 630 pieces of 2-inch x 10-inch x 18-foot lumber. If you were to put these end to end, they would stretch for approximately 11,340 feet, or a little over two miles. And all of it was pulled by a 1964 DCO International Emeryville. Senn Trucking, Inc. of Newberry, South Carolina, has been hauling loads like this since 1955. *Nichols Studio*

From Ohio to New Jersey and New York, SUWAK Trucking Co. of Washington, Pennsylvania, operated as a regular route common carrier. In 1977, it had a fleet of 150 tractors and 300 trailers. This International Fleetstar 2000 tractor and Ohio trailer show a sample of the equipment used by SUWAK in 1966. *Observer Publishing Co.*

Some trucks and trailers were designed for regular freight hauling and others for special purposes. This 1966-era International Fleetstar 2000 was one for regular use but the unknown brand trailer looks like it could be a bulk feed trailer. *Detroit Diesel*

This Canadian rig includes different makes of tractor and trailer. Atomic Transfer, Ltd. of Winnipeg, Manitoba, owns this 1966-era Hayes tractor and Can-car reefer trailer. Both pieces were manufactured in Canada. Atomic has been around since 1946. *Atomic Transfer, Ltd.*

Since 1937, Miller Transporters, Inc. of Jackson, Mississippi, has been transporters of liquid and dry bulk commodities through the continental United States. The 7000 White tractor and the compressed gas tank trailer shown here are examples of the many different types of tank trailer rigs that Miller had in its fleet. *E. H. Jaffe Photography*

Floyd & Beasley Transfer Co. of Sycamore, Alabama, served its home state plus Georgia, South Carolina, and Tennessee with a fleet of 139 tractors and 358 trailers. The White 7000 and Fruehauf trailer was one unit in the fleet in 1966. *Floyd & Beasley Transfer Co.*

It was a long haul from North Carolina to the West Coast. B&P Motor Lines of Hazelwood, North Carolina, started in 1956, and 10 years later used this White 7000 tractor and Black Diamond produce van on its West Coast run. *Black Diamond Trailer Co.*

Wearing cool sunglasses and a big smile makes this unidentified driver look very happy with his job. The big White-Freightliner tractor pulled two identical late-1950s Fruehauf trailers for Spector Freight System of Chicago. Notice that in this 1966 photograph, the trailers still carry the merger name of Spector-Mid States. *Caterpillar Engine Co.*

H. F. Johnson Transportation, Inc. of Billings, Montana, was a tank carrier from Big Sky country. A group shot of five White-Freightliners with tank bodies and pull-trailers shows what the fleet was like in 1967. *Ernie Ellesch*

W. S. Hatch Co. of Woods Cross, Utah, had a fleet of truck-trailer combinations as well as tractor-trailers. Different makes of trucks and many different types of trailers made Hatch a versatile carrier. This White-Freightliner with a dump body and dump pull-trailer operated in the western part of the country. *W. S. Hatch Co.*

McLean Trucking Co. of Winston-Salem was one of the biggest carriers in the South. Like many other companies, McLean's expansion came with the purchase of a number of trucking companies, including Hayes Freight Lines and Chicago Express, Inc. This gave McLean operating rights in the eastern half of the country. The total fleet was more than 1,500 tractors and 2,300 trailers. In 1966, one of those units was a White 7400 TBD and a Fruehauf trailer, pictured here. McLean was a big user of Whites and GMC Trucks. *White Motor Co.*

As a Canadian carrier, Provost Cartage Co., Ltd. of Montreal, Quebec, would have had slightly different rigs from those used in the United States. This White 7000 tractor is ready to pull a set of Fruehauf tank trailers. Provost started in 1927 and built up a fleet of more than 300 rigs. At this period, this type of doubles was not seen in the United States. *Provost Cartage Co., Ltd.*

One of the smaller California tank carriers was Gray Truck Co. of Vernon, California. This brand-new 1966 Peterbilt is pulling a petroleum tank trailer. *Gray Truck Co.*

Jones Truck Lines, Inc. of Springdale, Arkansas, ran between the Gulf and the Great Lakes. This orange-and-black International CO 4000 tractor and American trailer was one rig in the fleet. *Jones Truck Lines, Inc.*

Whitfield Tank Lines, Inc. of El Paso was one of many tank carriers in Texas. Whitfield started in 1943 and operated in the southwestern part of the country. One of the trucks in the fleet was this 1966 Peterbilt with tank body and tank pull-trailer. *Brian Williams*

West Coast travelers would come across many trucks running for Los Angeles-Seattle Motor Express (LASME) of Seattle. LASME started in the 1930s. In 1966, this Kenworth K100 tractor and matching set of Brown doubles was part of the fleet. *LASME*

What looks to be the first truck in the fleet is this 1966 International CO 4000 tractor and Wilson Possum-belly livestock trailer. F. L. Cruse Livestock Transport is the proud owner of Unit No. 1. *Woodworth Photography*

The huge parking lot of this sports complex in the San Francisco area was more than big enough to accommodate this rig for a picture session. Pacific Intermountain Express, Inc. (P-I-E) of Oakland, California, picked an ideal spot for this FL 700 Mack tractor and matching set of Trailmobile trailers to be in the limelight. P-I-E also had FL 700 Mack cab-over-engine tractors in tandem axles that were used mostly on eastern routes to pull 40-foot trailers. *Norton Pearl Photography*

Who had the honors of moving people's household goods from Maine to Florida? It was none other than S. Malatesta and Sons Moving and Storage of Paterson, New Jersey, and Hialeah, Florida. The traveling billboard was a colorful over-the-road sales piece. As can be seen, the 7000 White tractor and Kentucky drop-frame moving van trailer were in Florida at the time of this photo shoot. *Tierney & Killingsworth, Inc.*

In 1985, Provost Cartage, Inc. of Montreal, Quebec, had a tanker hauling business that covered all the Canadian provinces and the continental United States. Hauling all kinds of bulk commodities required a variety of different tank trailers in two different forms due to the fact that the weight and length laws were different from Canada to the United States. This late-1960s combination is a 7000 White tractor with two Fruehauf tank trailers, probably used for hauling gasoline. *Henry Koro Photographer*

When it comes to hauling bulk commodities, the first thing that leaps to mind is anything liquid that needs to be hauled in a tank trailer. Bulk hauling also includes things like bagged cement, however. Since Provost Cartage, Inc. was a bulk hauler, it not only had tank trailers for hauling liquid commodities, but also flatbed trailers for hauling bagged bulk commodities. Here we have another 7000 White no-sleeper tractor with matching Fruehauf flatbed trailers, probably used for hauling bagged cement. *Fernand Lapare Studio*

Another bulk hauler in the later 1960s was Mitchell Transport, Inc. of Cleveland, Ohio. Mitchell was a contract hauler for Lehigh Portland Cement Co., although the Butler tank trailer hooked to the White 4000 tractor here is not used for hauling bulk cement. Mitchell later became part of the Leaseway system. *Mitchell Transport, Inc.*

Chicago seemed to be the home base of a good number of refrigerated carriers, including Distributors Service Co. Distributors hauled meat and frozen foods from the Chicago area to a lot of the large cities in the mid-Atlantic area, as can be seen on the side of the trailer. The K100 Kenworth tractor and the Highway reefer trailer show how most of the company's trucks were painted. *Oscar & Associates Photography*

Dump trailers usually haul gravel, sand, dirt cinders, and similar loads. In this case, Iron and Metal Trucking Service, Inc. of Detroit has leased this White-Freightliner and set of Fruehauf dump trailers from Bob Papahk of Dearborn, Michigan, to haul scrap iron. This unit uses a typical Michigan-type setup of 11 axles. *Neil Sherff*

With 13 axles and 50 tires, this rig could haul 130,000 pounds of steel coils down the highway. Pulling this sizable load for Michigan Transportation Co. of Dearborn, Michigan, is a 1966 Marmon tractor. The Michigan truckers seem to have their own breed of rigs that works great for them. *Detroit Diesel*

Missouri-Pacific Railroad had its own truck fleet called MO-PAC. This 1966 International Fleetstar 2000 is hooked up to a set of Trailmobile doubles. Missouri-Pacific Truck Lines, Inc. of St. Louis, Missouri, covered the midsection of the country from Texas to Nebraska with a fleet of 385 tractors and 1,340 trailers. This photo was taken at the Houston, Texas, terminal. *Missouri-Pacific Truck Lines, Inc.*

Bend Portland Truck Service, Inc. of Portland, Oregon, ran this 1966 Kenworth K-100 combined with a set of Trailmobile doubles. BP was not a very large carrier, but it offered the same good service as the large carriers. *Herb Perkins*

This photo was taken at the time IML Freight, Inc. of Salt Lake City, Utah, was expanding its operation to the East Coast. This 1967 White 7000 was owned by Ecklar-Moore Express, Inc. of Lexington, Kentucky, and it was pulling a set of double trailers, one Trailmobile, and one Strick for IML Freight, Inc. At this time, Ecklar Moore Express was part of the IML operation. *Belford Studios*

Many companies pushed the length laws to their limits. Denver-Chicago Trucking Co., Inc. was one of the companies that took advantage of them and used this K-100 Kenworth tractor to pull these Trailmobile twin 40-foot reefers. *Denver-Chicago Trucking Co., Inc.*

By 1967, Pacific Intermountain Express Co. was a coast-to-coast carrier. This FL Mack western tractor and Trailmobile doubles were the type of equipment P-I-E used in its operation as far east as Ohio. The Mack FL westerns with sleeper cabs and tandem axles were used east of Ohio because Pennsylvania did not allow doubles. *Brian Williams*

One of the many divisions of Consolidated Freightways, Inc. was the bulk commodities division. Its territory was the continental 48 states plus Mexico and Canada, through Canadian Freightways, Ltd. This 1966 White-Freightliner with petroleum tank body and pull-trailer was typical of the equipment used in Consolidated's western territory. *Consolidated Freightways, Inc.*

Over the years, Spector Freight System, Inc. of Chicago was mainly a user of Whites, Fords, or Internationals. However, it did have some Peterbilts with Caterpillar diesel engines, and was a heavy user of Fruehauf trailers, as shown. *Caterpillar*

Canadian carriers were familiar with Dromedary rigs. White Pass Transportation Co., Ltd. ran this Canadian Kenworth with a Trailmobile Dromedary and a Trailmobile trailer. *Ron Adams collection*

Although the make of the truck and the trucking company name are the same, they were not connected in any way. Brockway Bulk Service of Somerville, New Jersey, got its start in 1930. The Brockway tractor and bulk tank trailer was one of the units in the fleet. *Brockway Bulk Service*

Southwest Marketing Association of Fort Worth, Texas, was a farm co-op that hauled nationwide with sharp-looking rigs like this black-and-yellow Peterbilt tractor and Hobb reefer trailer. *Don Lloyd Photo*

Dahlen Transport, Inc. of St. Paul, Minnesota, had both tank and van trailers. With a fleet of 250 tractors and 400 trailers, it covered the area of 36 states east of the Rocky Mountains in 1981. Here we have one of its earlier trucks. This 1967 International Fleetstar 2000 is pulling a compressed-gas tank trailer. *Detroit Diesel*

Canadian carrier Atomic Transfer, Ltd. of Winnipeg, Manitoba, used this 1967 White-Freightliner tractor with a Can-Car reefer trailer. The green-and-black Atomic trucks could be seen throughout Canada. *Ralf Lilje-Gren*

Until 1968, the biggest cab available was a 96-inch one. Then White-Freightliner brought 104-inch Vanliner models to the market. Neptune World Wide Moving Co. of New Rochelle, New York, leased one of the new Cat-powered Vanliners to pull a Brown drop-frame moving trailer. Notice the extended bumper and two sets of air horns. *Neptune Moving Co.*

The White-Freightliner Vanliner seemed to be popular with drivers who were leased to moving companies. Welch Transfer and Storage Co. of Twin Falls, Idaho, agent for Mayflower Transit Co., had a Vanliner to pull one of its furniture trailers. *Dudly Studio*

Kings County Truck Lines, Inc. of Tulare, California, had both reefer and tank trailers for hauling milk and food products. Founded in 1940, the company had 111 tractors and 242 trailers by 1991. In 1968, this White-Freightliner tractor pulled a matching set of Brenner milk tankers. The Kings County colors were red and cream yellow. *Kings County Truck Lines, Inc.*

Trimac Transportation Services, Ltd. of Calgary, Alberta, had a number of companies operating under it. In 1991, Trimac's fleet numbered 337 trucks, 375 tractors, and 2,087 trailers of various types. Part of that fleet was Municipal Tank Lines, Ltd. of Clarkson, Ontario, as seen in this 1968 photo of a White-Freightliner with a set of Fruehauf Canadian-style double tankers. Municipal was established in 1955. *Trimac Tranportation Services, Ltd.*

In 1966, Ford introduced its new W1000 series cab-over-engine tractor that replaced the previous "H" Series of the mid-1960s. Denver-Chicago Trucking Co. of Denver, Colorado, purchased some of these Ford 1000 tractors and Strick trailers. That same year, Time Freight, Inc., Los Angeles-Seattle Motor Express, and Denver-Chicago Trucking Co. merged into one carrier and became known as Time-DC, with headquarters based in Lubbock, Texas. This tractor was purchased just before the mergers took place. *Denver-Chicago Trucking Co.*

Eastern Canada had many trucking companies, some of whose territories reached clear across Canada to the Pacific and others of which operated more regionally. One of those eastern companies was Husband Transport, Ltd. of London, Ontario. To cover this territory, there was a fleet of 320 tractors and 800 trailers and a network of 20 terminals. One of the units in the fleet was this Dodge 1000 Series tractor and Fruehauf trailer. The tractor could have been Detroit Diesel powered. *Fred Muscat Photography*

Florida was one of the few states allowing 40-foot double trailers-but only on the Florida Turnpike. S. Malatesta & Sons took advantage of the two-for-one operation. It must have been a beautiful sight to see a rig come down the road looking like two moving billboards with this Chevrolet Titan 90 tractor and two Dorsey moving van trailers. *S. Malatesta & Sons*

This shows a three-way deal. Larry Banks of Cortland, New York, leased his 1968 Brockway tractor to Safeway Truck Lines of La Paz, Indiana, which pulled a Strick reefer trailer owned by Midwest Emery Freight System of Chicago. Safeway was owned by Midwest Emery. In 1981, the company had 1,572 tractors and 1,746 trailers consisting of reefers, vans, tankers, and flatbeds. *Brockway Motor Truck Co.*

This was taken at the time when Red Star Express Lines, Inc. of Auburn, New York, was completing delivery of 339 new trailers and 77 new tractors in 1969. This White 9000 and Strick 45-foot open-top trailer were part of the new equipment. The man standing beside the new rig is John Bisgrove, the company president. *Transport Topics*

Another Canadian carrier was Overland Express, Ltd. of Mississauga, Ontario. It had terminals throughout Ontario, in Buffalo, New York, and Detroit. The fleet consisted of 374 tractors, such as this 1969 W-1000 Ford, and 940 trailers, such as this Fruehauf. *Overland Express, Ltd.*

Dromedary bodies were used in almost any kind of hauling, such as vans, tanks, livestock, flatbed, and furniture rigs. This van Dromedary body was on a 1968 K-100 Kenworth pulling a Trailmobile trailer for Blue Eagle Truck Lines of Highland Park, Illinois. *Neil Sherff*

When a carrier was hauling any kind of dangerous freight, placards had to be placed on both tractor and trailer. Tri-State Motor Transit, Inc. of Joplin, Missouri, hauled ammunition and explosives. Placards were placed on both the tractor, a 1969 White-Freightliner with a Dromedary body, and on the Fruehauf trailer. The serviceman is probably checking the complete rig before it departs on its run. This was the routine of many carriers. *Tri-State Motor Transit, Inc.*

Stewart Transport, Inc. of Manchester, New Hampshire, was not a very large carrier in the 1960s. But with only about 6 tractors and 15 trailers, it did offer direct service to 15 states. One of those rigs was this 300 Series Brockway tractor and Dorsey trailer. *Stewart Transport, Inc.*

Double trailers were always a very familiar sight on the western and midwestern highways. One of the many companies who used them was Centralia Cartage Co. of Centralia, Illinois. The W-1000 Ford and the matching Fruehauf double trailers make for a beautiful picture.
Spieth Studios

From the sunny state of Florida comes refrigerated carrier Clay Hyder Trucking Lines, Inc. of Auburndale, which has been around for a good number of years. This is a circa 1969 White-Freightliner tractor and Timpte reefer trailer. *Clay Hyder Trucking Lines, Inc.*

One of the biggest and busiest refrigerated carriers was Curtis, Inc. of Denver, Colorado. Hauling products requiring refrigeration was a Curtis specialty. The trucks leased to Curtis, such as this Kenworth tractor and Utility trailer, shows the kind of sharp-looking equipment that was in its fleet. Wiebusch of Broken Bow, Nebraska, was the owner of this truck. Curtis, Inc. covered almost every state in the country. *Neil Sherff*

National Carriers, Inc. of Liberal, Kansas, hasn't always been a refrigerated carrier-early in its history the company also hauled livestock with trucks such as this K-100 Kenworth tractor and American livestock trailer in 1968. Today the company has a very large fleet of sharp-looking equipment and is known as "The Elite Fleet." *American Trailers*

By the late 1960s, some western companies were experimenting with triple trailers. Garrett Freightlines of Pocatello, Idaho, put this front-wheel-drive White-Freightliner tractor to work pulling one Comet, one Fruehauf, and one Brown trailer. Today, some western states allow triples. The rear axle was also a drive axle. *Freightliner Corp.*

Trucks with a full trailer were a rare sight on Pennsylvania highways. In 1969, H. W. Tayntons, Inc. of Wellsboro took delivery of six of these units. The truck is a Mack and the body and trailer are both Stricks. The 20-foot body and 26-foot trailer gave the rig 2,760 cubic feet of loading space. The body and trailer totaled 46 feet, which was a step ahead of the 40-foot trailers. *Transport Topics*

Willis Shaw Frozen Express, Inc. ran White-Freightliners and Trailmobile reefer trailers such as this one in 1969. By 1976, Willis Shaw had more than 400 of these units traveling on the American highways. *Ray Watson Photography*

Convoy Co. of Portland, Oregon, was an auto hauler in the Northwest since the 1930s. This "sporty" load of sports cars is being hauled by a Dodge L-1000 Series tractor. The rig was one of the many different setups used to haul vehicles in the Convoy fleet. *Ackroyd Photography, Inc.*

When you're in the heavy hauling business, you can expect oversized pieces of cargo. C&H Transportation Co., Inc. of Dallas always took on the challenge, even three of the world's largest tires by Goodyear. This 1969 International Transtar 4070 had the honor of hauling this load on a low-bed trailer. In 1981, C&H had a fleet of 1,500 tractors and 2,900 trailers working among 39 terminal throughout 49 states. *C&H Transportation Inc.*

Transamerican Freight Lines, Inc. of Detroit was among the top 10 motor carriers for many years. In 1977, it had a fleet of more than 1,200 tractors and 1,840 trailers of various types. It had a Steel and a Reefer Division with terminals from Texas to Nebraska and throughout the Midwest, into New England, and the South. This F-600 Mack tractor and van trailer were part of the late-1960s fleet. *Transamerican Freight Lines, Inc.*

By the late 1960s, longer trailers were becoming a reality. The larger trucking companies were usually the first ones to venture into new products. Transcon Lines, Inc. in El Segundo, California, served 36 of the 48 continental states. The fleet consisted of 777 tractors and more than 3,400 trailers in 1981. This late-1960s White-Freightliner tractor is pulling a 45-foot Pike rack-side trailer. The Transcon System was made up of 98 terminals coast to coast. *Transcon Lines, Inc.*

The route between Denver and Chicago seemed to be a busy one for refrigerated carriers! Scott Truck Lines, Inc. of Denver hauled a lot of meat and meat by-products between these two cities. One of the rigs the company used was this 1969 White-Freightliner tractor and American reefer trailer. For loads bound for east of Chicago, Scott interlined with various carriers. *Scott Truck Lines, Inc.*

CHAPTER SEVEN
THE STRUGGLE FOR SURVIVAL IN THE 1970S

The consolidation in the trucking industry throughout the 1950s and 1960s would continue in the 1970s, though in some cases for different reasons. With the fuel crisis of the early 1970s and a sluggish economy for most of the decade, trucking companies, owner-operators, and truck manufacturers were forced to find ways to survive. In some cases, that meant selling out to a competitor.

Truck manufacturers continued their progress. Kenworth followed White Freightliner's lead and came out with its version of a supersize cab to compete with the Vanliner. The Kenworth VIT measured 108 inches, 4 inches larger

than the Vanliner. Next came Peterbilt with its supersize cab measuring 110 inches, the biggest in the industry. A few other models to come were the White Road Boss and the Road Commander. GMC introduced the new General, and Diamond REO came out with the Raider and the Royal cab-over-engine.

Three names disappeared from the truck manufacturing scene: Hayes Trucks, Brockway, and Diamond REO. Diamond REO would later return under new ownership. Hayes and Brockway were taken over by Mack Trucks and discontinued in 1976.

Global Van Lines, Inc. of Orange, California, has been moving household goods nationwide and worldwide since 1948. The two-tone blue fleet had 509 tractors and 742 trailers traveling the country's highways. This International Transtar tractor and Highway furniture trailer are circa 1970. *Ron Adams collection*

A load of brand-new cars and pickup trucks are ready to roll to their happy customers. The hauler was Convoy Company of Portland, Oregon. Convoy had a mixed fleet of trucks, including this circa 1970 White-Freightliner. *Ackroyd Photography, Inc.*

This early-1970s Autocar tractor and Fruehauf gasoline tank trailer belonged to Provost Cartage, Inc. of Montreal, Quebec. *Provost Cartage, Inc.*

In 1976, the 25-year sales agreement between White and Freightliner expired, and Freightliner went back on its own. Both companies continued to steadily grow.

The manufacturers were always experimenting for ways to improve fuel mileage. Two such ways were aerodynamic nose cones for trailers and air shields for tractors.

Among the trucking companies that used these mighty new steeds, consolidation continued, in large part due to the difficult economic times of the decade. Some of these mergers and buyouts included Central Motor Lines by Akers Motor Lines, Associated Transport by Eastern "On The Ball" Freightways, Brady Motor Freight by Smith Transfer Corp., Dohrn's Transfer by Halls Motor Transit Co., ET&WNC Transportation Co. by Red Ball Motor Freight, Gateway Transportation Co. by Maislin Bros. of Canada, Hennis Freight Lines by Spector Freight System, Navajo Freight Lines by ABF, Dunn Freight Lines by Maislin Bros., R-C Motor Lines by Eastern Express, Jones Transfer Co. by Cooper Jarrett Motor Freight, Western-Gillette Transport by Roadway Express, Pic Walsh Freight Co. by Gateway Transportation Co., Wooster Express by North Penn Transfer, and Werner-Continental by Halls Motor Transit, Inc.

This circa 1970 White-Freightliner tractor and matching Fruehauf double trailers is an American-style rig from Canada. Motorways, Ltd. of Coquitlani, British Columbia, operated its fleet from the Canadian Pacific Coast to as far east as Montreal. *Motorways, Ltd.*

Over the years, Garrett Freightlines has always had nice equipment. The International 4300 tractor and Utility reefer trailer are one unit in a fleet of 487 tractors and 1,783 trailers that covered 11 western states through 64 terminals. *Garrett Freight Lines*

This Diamond REO, shown here pulling a Fruehauf reefer trailer, would have been a new truck in the market in 1970. Although there is no identification of the tractor showing ownership, it is believed to have been owned by R. A. Crawford Trucking Service of Adelphi, Maryland. *Al Salter Photography*

In 1970, Mason and Dixon Lines, Inc. of Kingsport, Tennessee, converted one of its 40-foot vans into a mobile classroom pulled by an F-600 Mack tractor. *Transport Topics*

In the late 1960s and early 1970s, western carriers started to develop tractor-trailer combinations unique to the region. W. S. Hatch Co. of Woods Cross, Utah, used this White-Freightliner tractor and Fruehauf Pneumatic Airslide trailer with a second trailer to haul a payload of up to 37 tons. The rig was 83 feet long, had a gross weight of 55 tons, and transported dry granular. A dusting of snow blankets the rig. *W. S. Hatch Co.*

Utah carrier F&B Truck Lines, Inc. of Salt Lake City was classified as a heavy hauler throughout the western states. The colors of the F-B trucks were blue and gold. This White-Freightliner tractor is using a gooseneck dolly to help transport its heavy object. *F-B Truck Lines, Inc.*

In eight mid-Atlantic and southern states, vehicles keep running thanks to O'Boyle Tank Lines, Inc. of Washington, D.C. Founded in 1932, O'Boyle has been delivering petroleum products for 37 years. This is an R-600 Mack tractor and Heil tank trailer. *Photos by Marler*

Nashua Motor Express, Inc. of Nashua, New Hampshire, had only two terminals, one in Boston, and one in Nashua. A total of 32 tractors and 55 trailers worked between the two terminals. The U Model Mack tractor and Strick trailer was one unit of the fleet. *Nashau Motor Express, Inc.*

This brand-new Kenworth tractor and Trailmobile reefer trailer were on the road for Clay Hyder Trucking Lines of Auburndale, Florida. The new Hyder graphics make for a nice appearance. *Clay Hyder Trucking Lines, Inc.*

New trucking companies are born almost every day. Most of them start as a one-truck operation and others may start with the purchase of a small fleet of tractors and trailers. In 1963, Golden West Freight Lines, Inc. of Bakersfield, California, started its operation hauling general freight and bulk commodities. The size of the fleet is not known, but approximately 10 years later in 1973, this International Transtar tractor and matching Fruehauf 27-foot double trailers were part of the fleet. *Golden West Freight Lines, Inc.*

These double 40-foot rigs were a big advantage for the companies that operated them. It meant hauling twice as much freight with one driver. The Ohio, Indiana, and Massachusetts Turnpikes and the New York State Thruway were the highways they were run on. This was very handy for Dohrn's Transfer Co. On this run, this GMC Astro 95 has the job of pulling two Trailmobile trailers of dry freight. *Dohrn's Transfer Co.*

The western highway always seemed to be the experimental place for new types of combinations to better the operations for trucking companies. At first a few companies would try out the new combinations, and others would follow when the experiment worked. Garrett Freightlines of Pocatello, Idaho, is one of many western companies benefiting from using triples in its operations. A Mack Cruiseliner tractor is pulling three identical Comet trailers in this operation. *Garrett Freightlines, Inc.*

Rocor International was a holding company for various businesses. From 1973 to 1976, Rocor acquired 20 different trucking companies. O N C Fast Freight, Inc. of San Francisco purchased Southern California Freight Lines, Inc. of Los Angeles, as well as other smaller carriers, eventually becoming a coast-to-coast carrier with a fleet of more than 2,600 units. This is an International Transtar 4070 A with a matching set of Pike doubles. O N C later became part of McLean Trucking Co., Inc. *O N C Freight System*

Since 1919, Belger Cartage Service, Inc. of Kansas City, Missouri, has been a specialized carrier with a fleet of 140 tractors, 150 straight trucks, and 295 varied trailers. This rig is an International Transtar 4070 accepting delivery of three brand-new drop-deck trailers. *Belger Cartage Service, Inc.*

A number of fleets were leased to trucking companies by independent owners. This group of 46 1971 GMC Astro 95s was purchased by Tom Jordan Trucking and leased to Midwest Coast Transport, Inc. of Sioux Falls, South Dakota. Tom Jordan also leased trucks to other carriers. *Jelleme Photography*

This F-600 Mack tractor is pulling a set of Fruehauf double tankers as part of the Provost fleet in Canada. This kind of rig was always interesting to see because it was a different type of trailer setup than in the United States. *Provost Cartage Co.*

This Provost rig is a White Road Boss tractor pulling a flatbed trailer with a Canadian Tri-Axle spread. Since Provost was classified as a bulk hauler, the under-cover load is probably bagged cement. *Provost Cartage Co.*

Spector Freight System of Chicago continued to run double trains on the turnpikes and throughways into the 1970s. This Peterbilt cab-over-engine tractor is pulling two 44-foot trailers of unknown make. Around this time, Spector changed its colors from red to white. *Spector Freight System*

This clean-looking Spector rig, a White-Freightliner tractor and Monon trailer, was probably just purchased as part of a new fleet. *Spector Freight System*

When this photograph was taken in the early 1970s, double trailers were not yet legal coast to coast. Transcon Lines of El Segundo, California, used doubles wherever and whenever it could. More than 800 tractors and 3,600 trailers made up the Transcon fleet, which traveled among 102 terminals. This unit is a White-Freightliner tractor pulling a matching set of Strick wedge-van doubles. *Transcon Lines, Inc.*

Some trucking companies did two types of hauling. Widing Transportation Co. of Portland, Oregon, was a heavy specialized carrier and also hauled liquid bulk. The tank operation came when Widing took over St. Johns Motor Express (also of Portland), which was also a heavy specialized carrier. This is a White-Freightliner truck with a Kari-Kool body and a Kari-Kool pull-trailer. *Widing Transportation Co.*

During the mid-1960s, United Truck Lines and Buckingham Transportation Co. merged to become United-Buckingham, Inc. In 1964, Ringsby Truck Lines, Inc. of Denver, Colorado, purchased United-Buckingham and Norwalk Truck Lines to become Ringsby-United, Inc., a coast-to-coast carrier. The company had a dry freight operation, heavy hauling division, tanker division, and a reefer division. This White-Freightliner tractor and Strick trailer were used in the dry freight division. *Grissinger Studio*

Ringsby-United was always looking for ways to better its operation. These Strick double trailers are pulled by an FL700 Mack tractor. Double trailers have been around the western trucking scene since the 1930s. These trailers display the Ringsby-United logo, but notice that on the cab door, the Ringsby Truck Lines, Inc. decal is still being used. Sometimes it took several years until all the old graphics were removed and replaced with the new ones. *Ringsby-United, Inc.*

Lee Way Motor Freight, Inc. of Oklahoma City, Oklahoma, got its start in 1914. Over the years it expanded by acquiring a number of other truck lines. One of the bigger purchases it made was Texas-Arizona Motor Freight, Inc. of El Paso. This gave Lee Way operating rights to the West Coast. By 1977, Lee Way had 83 terminals stretching from California to Pennsylvania in the East and Atlanta in the South. A fleet of 544 tractors and 2,469 trailers did the freight hauling between these 83 terminals. This GMC Astro 95 tractor and Fruehauf trailer are typical equipment used in 1977. *Lee Way Motor Freight, Inc.*

With a total of 42 tires, checked and ready to roll, the F700 Mack tractor and its eight-axle tanker trailer are prepared to make deliveries. This type of rig was used only in Michigan and was owned by Refiners Transport and Terminal Corp. of Oregon, Ohio. It was established in 1939 and has intrastate rights in Illinois, Indiana, Michigan, Ohio, and Pennsylvania. Its interstate rights cover the continental United States Refiners Transport hauls commodities such as acids, liquid and dry chemicals, coal tar products, petroleum, and petroleum products. This trailer is probably used for hauling petroleum. *Refiners Transport Corp.*

Werner Transportation Co. of St. Paul, Minnesota, got its start in 1931, about the same time Continental Transportation Lines, Inc. of Pittsburgh was founded. In 1968, Werner purchased Continental and became known as Werner-Continental. This purchase extended service to the East Coast and up into Boston. Werner-Continental, Inc. was another carrier that benefited from the use of 40-foot double trailers. Here we see a White Road Boss tractor pulling two Strick van trailers. *Werner-Continental, Inc.*

Trucks hauling for Reimer Express Lines, Ltd. of Winnipeg, Manitoba, are familiar sights on the Canadian highways. These black, green, and white trucks made daily runs transporting all kinds of commodities. This 9000 Ford tractor and Fruehauf reefer trailer carried freight requiring refrigeration. *Reimer Express Lines, Ltd.*

Among the many companies operating in the Midwest was Dohrn's Transfer Co. of Rock Island, Illinois, serving Minnesota, Iowa, Missouri, Wisconsin, Illinois, Indiana, Kentucky, Michigan, and Ohio. It had a total of 27 terminals in the area and a fleet of 663 tractors and 1,010 trailers. One of those units was this White Road Boss and Trailmobile trailer. *Dohrn's Transfer Co.*

Transporting bulk commodities is a specialty for Provost Cartage, Inc. of Montreal, Quebec. Since 1927, Provost has served its customers not only with good service but with good reliability and the proper equipment to get the job done. Provost covers almost all of Canada and the continental 48 states hauling all kinds of bulk and liquid commodities. The White Road Boss tractor and Fruehauf tanker trailer represent one of the varieties of equipment used in the Provost fleet. *Provost Cartage, Inc.*

Some freight carriers depended solely on owner-operator equipment to haul for them. Hagen, Inc. of Sioux City, Iowa, was a refrigerated carrier that used owner-operators. Many of the owner-operator rigs were done up in excess chrome with a nice two-, three- and sometimes four-tone paint job. Equipment such as this pre-1974 Peterbilt tractor with a Timpte reefer trailer made a good impression on the driver as well as the company he pulled for. *Harry Patterson*

Travelers anywhere in Canada are likely to see the black, green, and white trucks of Reimer Express Lines, Ltd. of Winnipeg, whose route extends from the St. Lawrence to the Canadian Pacific Coast. This is an F-600 Mack tractor and Can-Car reefer trailer. *Reimer Express Lines, Ltd.*

Western Truck Lines and Cantlay and Tanzola, Inc. of Los Angeles have been hauling freight since the 1920s. After the merger with Gillette Motor Transport, the new name became Western-Gillette Motor Freight. The company ran a variety of equipment, including triples like these being pulled by a GMC Astro 95. In 1979 Western-Gillette, Inc. became part of the huge Roadway Express, Inc., which made Roadway a coast-to-coast carrier. *Western Gillette, Inc.*

Standing tall and looking at you head-on is this International Transtar 4270 tractor, pulling a matching set of Comet trailers. Garrett Freight Lines, Inc. was the owner of this rig. Years later Garrett became part of the ANR Freight System. *Garrett Freight Lines, Inc.*

A White-Freightliner tractor, two Strick and one Brown trailer make up this triple rig. The high western landscape make it look like an HO scale toy truck. IML Freight, Inc. of Salt Lake City was one of the many western companies that started running triples. *IML Freight, Inc.*

A Texas landscape forms the background for this White-Freightliner tractor and Fruehauf trailer. Red Ball Motor Freight, Inc. of Dallas served 12 southwestern and Gulf Coast states with a fleet of 995 tractors and 1,224 trailers through 59 terminals. Red Ball was founded in 1931 and 50 years later merged with Spector to became known as Spector-Red Ball Freight System. The merger created a fleet of 1,548 road and 2,258 city tractors and 5,669 road and 1,912 city trailers, and a total of 153 terminals and 94 terminals in the Special Commodities Division. *Red Ball Motor Freight, Inc.*

In the 1960s, East Texas Motor Freight of Dallas was a Gulf-Coast-to-the-Great-Lakes carrier. Like many other companies, E.T.M.F. expanded its operations and became a coast-to-coast carrier. The International Transtar 4070 and matching Trailmobile trailers show what the E.T.M.F. fleet was like in 1973. *E.T.M.F.*

Another East Texas Motor Freight rig is this GMC Astro tractor and matching Lufkin trailers. By 1977, E.T.M.F. had 946 tractors and 2,561 trailers in its fleet. E.T.M.F. always had the newest and most modern equipment. *E.T.M.F.*

Oversize loads require special trailers. Dan Barclay Heavy Hauling and Rigging of Lincoln Park, New Jersey, had the equipment to do this job-a 361 Brockway with a low-bed trailer only inches from the ground. This is but one of the many different types of trailers in the Barclay fleet. The red-and-green tractors are decked out with plenty of fancy pinstriping. *Dan Barclay Hauling & Rigging*

Hauling heavy and odd-shaped pieces of machinery and equipment often made for strange-looking rigs. The tractors were uniform but the equipment necessary for heavy hauling gave the rig the unusual look. Widing Transportation Co., Inc. of Portland, Oregon, used a long wheelbase FL700 Mack tractor to haul a heavy piece of construction machinery. *Ackroyd Photography, Inc.*

Any load that was wider or higher than normal had to be fitted with red flags as well as signs like "Wide Load" or "Oversize Load" or "Long Load." These loads often could be hauled only during certain hours of the day. International Transport, Inc. of Rochester, Minnesota, took all the precautions for the safety of the load while in transit. The White-Freightliner tractor and low-bed trailer are decked out with the necessary warning signs and flags. *International Transport, Inc.*

Riss and Company of Kansas City, Missouri, got its start during the Depression. The Riss system included 28 terminals from Colorado to Texas to Boston, plus 15 terminals for perishable cargo, with a fleet of 628 company-owned tractors and 1,290 trailers. Owner-operators also hauled freight throughout the system, including this White compact tractor with a set of double flatbeds. *Riss International*

Another Riss & Company rig is this White-Freightliner tractor and Trailmobile trailer. *Riss International*

When John Hall started his one-truck operation in 1922, he probably never dreamed that he would build a giant trucking company. Hall's Motor Transit Co. of Mechanicsburg, Pennsylvania, had a continuous growth over its 60-year history. From its first truck in 1922, Hall's company grew to have more than 7,000 units by 1980. Over the years, Hall's absorbed approximately 10 other carriers. This White Road Boss tractor and Trailmobile trailer are from the early 1970s. *Hall's Motor Transit Co.*

This W-WT 9000 Ford tractor and Copco trailer are moving right along-the truck driver looks like he has everything under control. Holland Motor Express, Inc. of Holland, Michigan, operated in six midwestern states. The fleet totaled 620 tractors and 1,078 trailers. *Holland Motor Express, Inc.*

This Red Ball Motor Freight, Inc. rig sports the older company color. The International Transtar tractor is pulling twin Trailmobile trailers. *Red Ball Motor Freight, Inc.*

Time-DC resulted from the merger of Time Freight, Inc. of Lubbock, Texas, Los Angeles-Seattle Motor Express, Inc., and Denver-Chicago Trucking Co. With 80 terminals, the company's combined fleet included 842 tractors and 3,586 trailers, among them this Kenworth tractor and set of Utility doubles. *Time-DC, Inc.*

The Trimac fleet was made up of several different trucking companies, including Canada's H. M. Trimble & Sons, Ltd. of Calgary, Alberta. In its fleet was this R-600 Mack tractor and Fruehauf bottom-dump trailer that hauled grain and fertilizer throughout the Trimac System. *Trimac, Inc.*

The Missouri-Pacific Truck Lines, Inc. of St. Louis was the line of the Missouri-Pacific Railroad (MO-PAC). This White Road Commander-2 was one of 385 tractors, and the Fruehauf trailer was one of 1,340 trailers, in the fleet. They were also connected with Texas & Pacific Motor Transport Co., also of St. Louis. *Missouri-Pacific Truck Lines, Inc.*

Jones Motor Co. of Spring City, Pennsylvania, was actually started in 1894, but the first truck was purchased in 1912. Starting out as Jones Drayage, it came a long way by purchasing other truck lines to expand its operating territory. This rig includes a U model Mack tractor and Gindy open-top trailer. *Jones Motor Co.*

This Ford L9000 tractor and Fruehauf trailer were among the 958 tractors and 1,902 trailers in the Jones fleet. The Jones territory covered New Hampshire in the East, Tennessee in the South, Iowa in the West, and many states in between. The freight handled in this area was done with a fleet of all types. *Jones Motor Co.*

Is there room for one more? For cars this size, no, but for the smaller cars of today, yes. You could fit 13-14 small cars on a rig like this. Motor Convoy Co., Inc. of Atlanta made the most of the available space that it could. This Louisville Ford is showing off its valuable cargo. *Motor Convoy Co., Inc.*

The name Key Line Freight, Inc. of Grand Rapids, Michigan, was somewhat new but the company was not. Darling Freight, Inc. started in the 1920s, and in the later years changed to Key Line Freight, Inc. The White Road Commander-2 and the Monon double trailers were part of a fleet of 400 tractors and 1,105 trailers. *Robinson Studio*

Black Ball Freight System of Seattle was another Rocor International-owned line. Lit up in the night is this International Transtar 4070 tractor with a matching set of Pike double trailers. *Black Ball Freight Service*

Back in the early 1970s, Consolidated Freightways decided to change the company colors. The White-Freightliner tractor and matching Trailmobile double trailers made up one unit in a fleet of more than 14,500 tractors, trailers, and trucks in 1977. In the background at the dock is a White-Freightliner half-cab used as a yard hustler. *Consolidated Freightways, Inc.*

New Penn Motor Express, Inc. of Lebanon, Pennsylvania, got started in 1931 with one truck, but today the total is 480 tractors and 1,125 trailers. This 1970s rig is a F-700 Mack tractor and Fruehauf trailer. *Lebanon Daily News*

Jones Truck Lines, Inc. of Springdale, Arkansas, has been around for many years. These orange-and-black trucks were a common sight on the highways from the Gulf to the Great Lakes. This International Transtar 4070 tractor is ready to haul with double trailers, one a Great Dane and one an unknown brand. *Jones Truck Lines, Inc.*

Fleet Transport Co., Inc. of Nashville, Tennessee, got its start in 1948 as a tanker hauler. Its operating terminals were mainly in the South, but the company served 27 states. This White Road Boss and Heil tanker operate out of Swift & Co. in Chattanooga, where this photo was taken on June 21, 1975, at the TVA power plant. *Fleet Transport Co., Inc.*

In 1976, some carriers painted trailers in honor of the United States Bicentennial. Pre-Fab Transit Co., Inc. of Farmer City, Illinois, made its contribution by showing Washington crossing the Delaware. Pre-Fab was a carrier that hauled building materials with a fleet of 450 tractors and 600 trailers through the contiguous 48 states. This bicentennial rig is a Chevrolet Titan 90 tractor and Trailmobile trailer. *Pre-Fab Transit Co., Inc.*

A little over 100 years ago, a horse and wagon company was the forerunner of Mushroom Transportation Co. of Philadelphia. In 1913, the company purchased its first truck, an Autocar. This 1978 R-700 Mack and Gindy trailer, with its red, orange, and black colors, is by far a lot different than old No. 1. *Mushroom Transportation Co.*

Florida's fruit and produce got shipped north by several Florida-based carriers, including Greenstein Trucking of Pompano Beach. This Kenworth VIT with its 108-inch cab and the Great Dane reefer trailer helped the company get the load to its destination on time, every time. *Ron Adams collection*

Central Freight Lines, Inc. of Waco, Texas, was founded in 1925 and grew through the years to cover the whole state of Texas with more than 4,000 units. Pictured here is a Ford 9000 Louisville tractor and Lufkin trailer. *Central Freight Lines, Inc.*

During the 1970s, some companies changed their image. Kroblin Refrigerated Express, Inc. of Waterloo, Iowa, changed its red-and-white trucks to the new sunshine colors look shown here. Kroblin had a variety of trailer types in its fleet. This White-Freightliner tractor is matched with a Fruehauf reefer trailer. Kroblin had a fleet of 455 tractors and 665 trailers that ran among 35 terminals stretching from Colorado to Maine. Kroblin started its operation in 1948. *Kroblin Refrigerated Express, Inc.*

In the 1970s, triple trailer operations became popular in the western states. Garrett Freightlines, Inc. of Pocatello, Idaho, was one of many companies operating triples. Garrett had various makes of tractors pulling the triples-in this case, an International Transtar is pulling three identical Comet trailers. The Garrett colors were always yellow and green. *Garrett Freight Lines, Inc.*

CHAPTER EIGHT

DEREGULATION IN THE 1980s

As big trucks rolled through the Reagan and Bush years of the 1980s, we saw trucking companies leave the trucking scene in a different way. A recession during the first few years of the decade hurt, but it was the deregulation of the industry in 1983 that carried the biggest wallop for the industry's established powers. Companies that expanded their operating territory in the decades prior by buying out other companies became victims during these turbulent times—many of them were the pioneers of the trucking industry. Long-heralded carriers such as P-I-E, TIME-DC, Wilson Freight Co., Transcon Lines, McLean Trucking Co., Halls Motor Transit Co., Spector Freight System, Navajo Freight Lines, Cooper Jarrett Motor Freight, and Smith Transfer Co., were swallowed up during the 1980s. They are gone but not forgotten.

In the early 1980s, there were big layoffs. This meant that the manufacturing companies were producing less of their products, which meant there was less to haul. Since many of these trucking giants hauled the same kinds of freight, there wasn't enough to go around for everyone, so some had to lose. Chapter 11 bankruptcy was the end result for these companies. Some of them hauled freight at the lowest possible rates that they could. Many loads were hauled just to break even so they could survive a little bit longer. Finally, it caught up with them and the last word was Chapter 11.

Still, other companies benefited from deregulation, and some of those are today's trucking giants. Werner Enterprises, J. B. Hunt, Schneider National, and U.S. Express Enterprises are just a few examples.

Truck manufacturers continued to respond to the need for better fuel mileage, and truck bodies became more aerodynamic. Kenworth hit the road first with its T-600, known as the "anteater." Others, such as Peterbilt, Freightliner, Mack, White, and International, followed. Some models had sloped hoods, side flarings, condo sleeper cabs, and had sloped or rounded roofs. One benefit of deregulation was that double trailers became legal in 48 states. This made it convenient for the coast-to-coast carriers. Where years ago there were eastern-type trucks and western-type trucks, the new rules made everything uniform. The length limits increased and brought on the use of 53-foot trailers, allowing specialty carriers like the auto haulers to haul more cars on one load.

Utility Trailer Co. designed a new type of trailer called the Taut-Liner in the early 1980s. This set of Taut-Liners is being pulled by a 1980 CL 9000 Ford, owned by Viking Freight System of San Jose, California. Viking was a coast-to-coast general freight carrier with a fleet of 1,102 tractors and 3,991 trailers plus 240 leased tractors and 520 leased trailers. *Ron Adams collection*

In the 1980s, car hauler trucks like this one were used nationwide instead of only in the western part of the country. Nu-Car Carriers, Inc. of Bryn Mawr, Pennsylvania, made the change to this type of rig, as did other eastern auto haulers. This International tractor and Delavan trailer was one of many in the fleet. Notice that on the nameplate in the grille, it says Nu-Car Carriers instead of International. *Doug Grieve*

This is the golden anniversary truck for Mason and Dixon Lines, Inc. of Kingsport, Tennessee. This 1982 Mack Cruiseliner tractor and set of Monon twin trailers are painted gold to commemorate the company's 50 years of service. This company was nicknamed the "Hand Shakers" because of the two men shaking hands, shown on the trailers. The two men, General Lee and General Grant, represented the joining of the North and South. *Mason & Dixon Lines*

Trade show displays and exhibits are moved frequently and often require special handling. Mural Transport, Inc. of Long Island City, New York, has specialized in moving exhibits and displays since 1930. A fleet of 283 tractors and 804 trailers do the transporting. This Kenworth K-100 tractor and unknown brand of trailer take time out to pose for a picture before moving on. *Bob Homan Photography*

Brasher Truck Co. of St. Louis, Missouri, got its start back in the 1910s or 1920s. Somewhere along the line, the company changed its name to Middlewest Freightways, Inc. In 1988, it was a general freight hauler operating in four midwestern states with a fleet of 65 tractors and 343 trailers. One of the Middlewest trucks is this White-Freightliner tractor and Pines open-top 45-foot trailer. *Middlewest Freightways, Inc.*

The name Freightways has been around since 1929. During the 1930s, the name Consolidated was added and the company became known as Consolidated Freightways, Inc. of Portland, Oregon. Years later, the main office was moved to Menlo Park, California. In 1960, C.F. became the second coast-to-coast carrier and the largest trucking company overall with the purchase of the Motor Cargo Co. of Akron, Ohio. In 1990, C.F. had a fleet of 8,231 tractors and 27,674 trailers serving the continental United States and Canada. White-Freightliner tractors were used systemwide because C.F. owned the Freightliner Corp. *Consolidated Freightways, Inc.*

This Kenworth tractor is pulling a set of Utility double trailers. This kind of rig was a common sight on the highways and routes served by Viking Freight System of San Jose, California. *Rick Manz*

The Rocky Mountains were a challenge for western trucking companies. Salt Creek Freightways, Inc. of Casper, Wyoming, picked a scenic spot to show off one of its Freightliner tractors and Trailmobile trailers. Salt Creek covered seven states in Big Sky country with 200 tractors and 493 trailers. *Salt Creek Freightways, Inc.*

Arkansas Best Freight System (ABF) of Fort Smith, Arkansas, has been around for many years. ABF became a big coast-to-coast carrier in 1979 when it took over Navajo Freight Lines of Denver, Colorado. This Freightliner tractor and set of doubles is one of 3,421 tractors and 11,665 trailers. Buying out several carriers over the years helped to make the giant trucking company what it is today. *John Hiestand*

Roadway Express, Inc. of Akron, Ohio, is another trucking giant. Roadway became a coast-to-coast carrier in the late 1970s when it took over Western Gillette Transport of Dallas. With Roadway's fleet of 3,367 tractors and 28,975 trailers, not much area of the country goes untouched. This White tractor and Fruehauf and Pines double trailers are part of the large fleet. *Rick Manz*

Illinois-California Express (I-C-X) of Denver, Colorado, got its start during the Depression. For 50 years, it was hauling freight in the West and eventually working its way as far east as Ohio. This White tractor with a set of double trailers was part of a 2,500-unit fleet. In 1984, its doors closed due to financial problems. *John Hiestand*

Building a trucking company into a $90 million operation in 20 years is quite an accomplishment. That's exactly what Swift Transportation Co. of Phoenix, Arizona, did since its start in 1968. Being a nationwide carrier of general freight, refrigerated products, and building materials, it had a fleet of 952 tractors and 1,043 trailers in 1990. This White tractor and set of flatbed double trailers made up one of the various types of units used in Swift's operation. *Rick Manz*

Bekins Van Lines Co. of Hillside, Illinois, has been around for many years. The household goods-hauling business has almost always had lease-operator tractors pulling company or agent-owned trailers. Bekins always seemed to be the moving company that attracted a lot of the lease operators who liked their equipment extra fancy. Here we see a Kenworth Aerodyne tractor with an add-on custom-built sleeping and living quarters pulling a furniture-hauling trailer. *Neil Sherff*

The Pacific Northwest had a lot of smaller but well-established carriers. Since 1926, Puget Sound Truck Lines, Inc. of Seattle has been hauling forest products, wood chips, and general freight. Its fleet of 91 tractors, 520 trailers, and 179 pieces of leased equipment was getting the job done for its satisfied customers. Here we have a Kenworth tractor pulling an Alloy van trailer for general freight hauling. *Puget Sound Truck Lines, Inc.*

Trucking companies usually stuck with the color of the trucks that they originally started with. However, some companies felt the need for a change, as was the case with P-I-E Nationwide, Inc. of Jacksonville, Florida. For many years, the P-I-E colors were red, but with the merging of Ryder Truck Lines into the P-I-E system, they felt a need for change. This Freightliner tractor shows the new blue color and the triples show the new graphics with P-I-E red and Ryder blue. *Rick Manz*

The New York State Thruway and the Massachusetts Turnpike benefited companies like Boston-Buffalo Express, Inc. of Syracuse, New York, which ran double-40s to haul canned goods, paper, foodstuffs, and general freight. Over the 20 years since its founding in 1969, Boston-Buffalo built up a fleet of 87 tractors and 154 trailers. This unit is an R Model Mack tractor pulling two Great Dane reefer trailers. *Bob Baciulis*

Hauling chemicals, printed matter, household cleaners, and paper products requires certain kinds of trailers. K-B Transport, Inc. of Rochester, New York, founded in 1978, has a fleet of 42 tractors and 200 trailers, such as this International tractor and Bar-Bell tank trailer. The trailer fleet consists of vans, reefers, and tankers. *Bob Baciulis*

Consolidated Freightways of Menlo Park, California, changed its colors to white with red-and-green stripes. For many years, C.F. had only Freightliners in the fleet. The pattern has changed, as evidenced by this International tractor with double trailers. This tractor is one of 150 of these Internationals the company had in 1985. *Mel Carnahan*

Back in the 1940s and 1950s, not many western rigs would be seen in the East. As the Interstate system improved and expanded, more western trucking companies started hauling to the East Coast. May Trucking, Inc. of Payette, Idaho, hauled bulk commodities, general freight, and refrigerated since 1940. They also hauled to the East in the mid-1980s. This K-100 Kenworth tractor and Utility reefer trailer were used for hauling refrigerated foods. *Harry Patterson*

The western companies usually had long-wheelbase tractors. Arrow Transportation Co. of Seattle, had this International tractor and outside frame flatbed trailer with removable sides in its fleet. A headache rack (a metal rack behind the cab to protect the back of the cab from objects that might slide forward from the trailer) and a tool box were added accessories needed for the job. *Rick Manz*

ABF uses some Tri-Axle van trailers for hauling general freight, appliances, auto parts, and foodstuffs. This "R" model Mack, which is around 48 feet long, is the source of power to pull the Trailmobile Tri-Axle trailer. By 1989, the fleet is made up of 3,421 tractors and 11,665 trailers. *John Hiestand*

TNT is a holding company that owns a number of trucking companies throughout the United States and Canada, including Bestway Transportation Co. of Phoenix, Arizona. All the TNT companies carry the orange-and-white color scheme. The Freightliner tractor is one of 198 tractors, and the Fruehauf and Strick trailers are two of 383 trailers in the Bestway fleet. *Rick Manz*

It seems like the early 1930s were good years to get into the trucking business. Ward Trucking Corp. of Altoona, Pennsylvania, got its start in 1931, and is still going strong today. In 1991 it served five states with a fleet of 250 tractors and 431 trailers, including this GMC Brigadier tractor and Fruehauf double trailers. *Ward Trucking Corp.*

Loading to capacity is the name of the game in the car-hauling business. If Jack Cooper Transport Co. of Oklahoma City, Oklahoma, were to fill all its 948 units at 12 cars per unit, it could haul 11,376 automobiles on one trip. If each unit made one trip per week for one year, it would have hauled a total of 591,552 automobiles. This GMC Brigadier tractor is one in the fleet. *John Hiestand*

Commercial Carriers, Inc. of Bloomfield Heights, Michigan, a division of the Ryder Systems, is an auto hauler founded in 1934. By 1990 it had a fleet of 1,600 tractors and 1,788 trailers. This Kenworth auto hauler rig was assembled in Billings, Montana, in May 1989. *John Hiestand*

NW Transport Service, Inc. of Commerce City, Colorado, started in business in 1961, and over the course of the next 28 years built up a fleet of 927 tractors and 3,127 trailers to haul foodstuffs, auto parts, electronics, and paint. The NW unit pictured here is a Freightliner tractor with a set of Strick double trailers. *Rick Manz*

In 1965, Montgomery Tank Lines, Inc. of Summit, Illinois, started in business. It has terminals spotted across the country. Its prime authority as a contract carrier is to haul chemicals and related products, food and related products, and petroleum and related products between points in the United States. This company has many lease operators with sharp-looking equipment, such as this 379 Peterbilt tractor pulling a stainless steel tank trailer. *Neil Sherff*

Today, every trucking company is going for as much volume as it can get. Manufacturers make bodies bigger, using low-profile tires to stay within legal height limits. This truck-trailer combination was designed by RUAN Rentals, Inc. of Des Moines, Iowa. RUAN has almost always been a user of International trucks such as this cab-over-engine with a Fruehauf body and trailer. *RUAN Rentals, Inc.*

Builder Transport, Inc. of Camden, South Carolina, founded in 1962, hauls general freight, building materials, refrigerated solids, and liquids. In 1990, Builder Transport used a fleet of 968 tractors, 1,542 leased tractors, and 4,483 trailers such as this International tractor and Great Dane trailer. *Rick Manz*

Tri-State Motor Transit, Inc. of Joplin, Missouri, hauls with a wide variety of trailers in its fleet. The fleet includes 222 tractors, with 678 leased operators and more than 1,800 trailers. This particular unit is a lease operator's Freightliner tractor pulling a military load with one of Tri-States drop-deck trailers. *Harry Patterson*

Before deregulation in the 1980s, many companies were basically operating in small areas-about two, three, or four states. After deregulation, a lot of those companies expanded their area of operations. Brown Transport Corp. of Charlotte, North Carolina, operated in 14 southern and midwestern states, but expanded to the West Coast after deregulation. A fleet of 1,966 tractors and 4,791 trailers moved the freight throughout the Brown system. This W-900 Kenworth tractor with twin trailers was one of the many units used to move freight. Brown is no longer in business. *Rick Manz*

Many distribution centers had their own fleet of trucks. Along the Pacific Coast, Superior Fast Freight, Inc. of Seattle used this C Model Ford and Utility trailer. *Ron Adams collection*

In 1950, George Peters of Lenhartsville, Pennsylvania, started trucking for Daniels Motor Freight of Warren, Ohio, with his GMC tractor. In 1952, he and his brother Bill started hauling livestock on their own as Peters Bros. They hauled livestock for 30 years and some drivers made three round trips a week from Allentown to St. Louis and back. Toward the end of the livestock-hauling era, they started to get into the reefer-hauling business, which is their major operation today. Over the years, they had many trucks, one of which is this 1989 Western Star tractor and Timpte reefer trailer. *Ron Adams*

Hauling agricultural and refrigerated products can usually turn into cross-country runs. Sam Tanksley Trucking, Inc. of Cape Girardeau, Missouri, was classified as a refrigerated and agricultural carrier. In the later 1970s, many of the carriers started going to all-white tractors. The Peterbilt tractor and Dorsey reefer trailer here are dressed in patriotic colors. *Sam Tanksley Trucking, Inc.*

The 1960s saw new companies form, such as Continental Contract Carrier Corp. of City of Industry, California. Later on, "Contract" was eliminated from the name. The company was classified as a contract carrier of specified commodities hauling coast to coast. One of the trucks it ran was this International tractor and Theurer 48-foot trailer. *Continental Carrier Corp.*

Being a relatively new company of the 1980s, Roadway Package System (R.P.S.) was formed by the parent company Roadway Express, Inc. Owner-operators' tractors are used for pulling the R.P.S. trailers. The owner of this Kenworth tractor is John Hiestand of Elizabethtown, Pennsylvania. The original color was red, and it had a tandem axle when he was pulling for Mason Dixon Tank Lines, but R.P.S. required that all tractors be painted white. John ran out of the Harrisburg, Pennsylvania, terminal. This picture was taken in Lewisburg, Pennsylvania, in October 1989. *John Hiestand*

Like many companies, McLean Trucking Co., Inc. of Winston-Salem, North Carolina, started out as a one-truck operation and eventually grew into a trucking giant. Two big acquisitions McLean made were Hayes Freight Lines and Chicago Express, giving the company rights into the Midwest. This GMC Brigadier tractor and Trailmobile trailer are one in a fleet of more than 5,000 tractors and 9,000 trailers. *McLean Trucking Co., Inc.*

CHAPTER NINE

END OF A CENTURY IN THE 1990s

A lot of mergers that take place are of the kind in which a company might have a certain kind of operation similar to that of other companies. Company A sees that Company B is not quite as big, but that Company B has a really good, progressive business. Company A is very interested in the progressive growth of Company B, so meetings take place and Company A offers a good package deal to Company B. Both sides agree on the deal, and Company A takes over the operations of Company B, therefore expanding the operations of Company A into new areas of the country. Mergers such as this are happening every day.

The developments among tractors are increasing every so often. The biggest thing in tractor design is aerodynamics. Every over-the-road tractor is aerodynamically designed, and the T2000 Kenworth is the one that is probably the most aerodynamic tractor today. Every truck manufacturer comes up with new designs, not only with aerodynamics, but interior components as well. On-board computers, color TVs, and bigger sleeper boxes of up to 72 inches are becoming standard equipment. Just how far manufacturers can go with offering new engineering designs and interior components as we go into the new millennium remains to be seen.

There will always be challenges facing the trucking industry. What they will be in the years to come will be anybody's guess. Increasing the length of trailers, raising the weight, and legalizing triple trailers seem to be talked about as challenges for the twentyfirst century. Of course, our highway system must be able to withstand these elements when applied.

We are in the decade of aerodynamic trucks. Bigger and better engines for better fuel mileage have become standard equipment. Companies such as Roadway Express, Inc., Overnite Transportation Co., and Consolidated Freightways, have grown into giant nationwide trucking operations, holding on to their old customers and gaining new ones. For many companies, it was an uphill battle all the way, and they survived it all. From the day the first truck was manufactured up to today, the 100 years of trucks and freight carriers have helped to make our nation a better place to live.

For many years, Dromedary bodies were used only on cab-over-engine tractors. Today, some carriers are using Dromedary bodies on conventional tractors, such as this Freightliner for Boyle Transport, Inc. of Billerica, Massachusetts. This tractor is one of 35, along with 55 vans, reefers, and flatbeds, that allow Boyle to haul general freight, spices, printed matter, and military freight. *John Hiestand*

Swift Transportation Co. of Phoenix, Arizona, used a variety of equipment, including this Freightliner truck-trailer combination. Swift has hauled general freight, refrigerated products, and building materials since 1968. *Rick Manz*

For over 25 years, Roadway Express, Inc. of Akron, Ohio, ran terminal to terminal with one driver. In 1993, Roadway started using sleeper teams for long-run hauling. This picture was taken in Evanston, Wyoming. The Volvo White sleeper tractor pulling Wabash and Strick double trailers was on a run from Dallas to Seattle. *John Hiestand*

The four companies in the Con-Way Express system have been keeping up with the challenging pace of today's trucking industry. All four of the Con-Way companies intermix their equipment. The fleet of the Con-Way Southern Express of Portland, Oregon, consists of 462 tractors and 1,139 trailers. One of the units in the fleet is this L9000 Ford with matching double trailers. *John Hiestand*

Thirty years sounds like a very long time to be at something, but when you compare that time to 60 or 70 years, it's a rather short time. In this case, that's how long J. B. Hunt Transport, Inc. of Lowell, Arkansas, has been around. Since 1969, Hunt has worked its way to the top to be one of the nation's largest trucking companies. In 30 years, it built up a fleet of 4,241 tractors and 9,339 trailers. One unit of the fleet is this International tractor and 53-foot trailer. *John Hiestand*

Still around after 43 years, in 1989 Atomic Transportation System, Inc. of Winnipeg had a fleet of 188 trucks, 200 tractors, and 400 trailers to haul foodstuffs and perishables. One of those busy units is this CH Mack tractor and matching set of Fruehauf trailers. *Doug Grieve*

Hayes Transport, Inc. of Verona, Wisconsin, is a relatively new company. This well-maintained Peterbilt tractor and Utility reefer trailer are examples of the pride the company takes in keeping its equipment in good condition. *Neil Sherff*

Interstate Grocery Distribution System, Inc. owns its trucking company, Interstate Trucking of North Bergen, New Jersey. With a somewhat small fleet of 20 tractors and 25 trailers, this International S-2250 tractor and van trailer stay busy. *John Hiestand*

When Watkins Motor Lines, Inc. of Lakeland, Florida, started in 1932, it was mainly a refrigerated carrier. At one time it had several divisions, including Watkins Carolina Express and Watkins Texas Express. In 1981, Watkins had a fleet of 547 tractors and 949 refrigerated and dry freight vans hauling in 40 states. Ten years later, the fleet numbers 1,231 tractors-including leased tractors-and 2,851 trailers. This International tractor and Monon double trailers are leased. *Rick Manz*

Canadian carrier Sunbury Transport, Ltd. of Fredrickton, New Brunswick, hauls a lot of paper products in van trailers, but also has some reefer and flatbed trailers with a variety of different makes of tractors. This International tractor and Fruehauf trailer are one of the rigs in the Sunbury fleet. *Dick Copello*

Lee & Eastes of Seattle has been trucking in the Northwest since 1925. Starting out as a freight hauler, the company got into the tanker-hauling business around 1946. Today, with a fleet of approximately 16 tractors, 51 trucks, and 114 trailers, Lee & Eastes serves Washington, Oregon, and Idaho. This Peterbilt truck with tanker body and tanker pull-trailer hauls liquid petroleum and other liquid products. *Gary Morton, Inc.*

Arrow Transportation Co. of Portland, Oregon, has been hauling liquid chemicals, petroleum, and asphalt since 1931. It's still in operation today, hauling liquid products in five western states and British Columbia. This Kenworth tanker truck-trailer combination is one of many serving the Northwest. *Gary Morton, Inc.*

Delta Lines, Inc. of Emeryville, California, got its start way back in 1854 carrying freight on rafts. It wasn't until 1930, however, that Delta Lines started a trucking operation with two half-ton Fageols. Today's modern equipment in the Delta fleet includes a Ford CL9000 tractor and a set of Fruehauf double trailers. The name was changed to Delta California, Inc. in the 1970s, and in 1981 became part of Meridian Express Co. of Dallas. *Ron Adams collection*

Tudhope Cartage, Ltd. of Parry Sound, Ontario, uses this Canadian-style (different spread of axles than the United States) Western Star sleeper tractor and Hutchinson tank trailer to haul liquid petroleum throughout Ontario. *John Hiestand*

Here we have the exact same type of Western Star tractor and Hutchinson liquid petroleum tank trailers. A combination such as this is known as a "B" train, which has a fifth wheel on the end of the first trailer to hook up the second trailer to form the train. Tudhope Cartage, Ltd. of Parry Sound, Ontario, also has this rig in its fleet. *John Hiestand*

Groendyke Transport, Inc. of Enid, Oklahoma, is another in the long list of companies started during the Depression—in this case 1932. Some 67 years later, and still going strong, Groendyke has built a network of terminals in seven southwestern states. Its territory covers the 48 states with a fleet of 800 tractors—including lease operators—and 1,250 tanker trailers. This Freightliner tractor with tank trailer shows the kind of equipment in the Groendyke fleet. *John Hiestand*

Born of deregulation in the 1980s, Arkansas Freightways, Inc. of Harrison, Arkansas, serves the midwestern and southwestern part of the country. From its start in 1982 up to 1990, the company built up a fleet of 843 company tractors, 261 leased tractors, and 2,500 trailers. One of the units it runs is this International tractor with Fruehauf double trailers. *Arkansas Freightways, Inc.*

Shaffer Trucking Co., Inc. of New Kingstown, Pennsylvania, has been a refrigerated carrier since 1953. As of 1990, the fleet totaled 213 tractors, 554 trailers, and 160 leased tractors, such as this T600 Kenworth tractor and Utility trailer. *Dick Copello*

From its beginning in 1969, J. B. Hunt Transport, Inc. of Lowell, Arkansas, has been a general freight hauler. In 20 years, the Hunt fleet grew to a total of 4,241 tractors and 9,339 trailers before it started a flatbed division in the 1990s. Here we see an International tractor with a spread-axle trailer painted in the Hunt tan and orange. *Dick Copello*

Since household goods carriers have always been cross-country haulers, drivers are typically gone for weeks at a time. Over the years, sleeper cabs were almost a must for this type of hauling. North American Van Lines, Inc. of Fort Wayne, Indiana, offers its drivers units like this 377 Peterbilt with an extra large sleeper to be a home away from home while hauling with a Kentucky trailer. *Neil Sherff*

The small package-hauling business has picked up considerably over the last 25 years. Roberts Express, Inc. of Akron, Ohio, owned by the giant Roadway Express, entered the small package business in 1975. The fleet is all lease operators, making up a total of 854 trucks. This CH Mack represents the kind of equipment that makes up the fleet. *Neil Sherff*

Since deregulation, many of the old pioneer trucking companies have gone by the wayside. One that is still around is Willig Freight Lines, Inc. of San Francisco. Since 1923, Willig had been hauling freight over the California highways from San Francisco to Los Angeles. In 1991, Willig had a fleet of 528 tractors and 1,140 trailers. At the time of this picture (1991), the basic fleet consisted of Freightliner tractors such as this one, which is pulling double trailers. *Rick Manz*

This looks more like a storage tank than an over-the-road trailer. But in Canada they made them big and used them over the road. Provincial Tankers, Ltd. (P.T.L.) of Toronto used this superliner Mack tractor to pull the King tank trailer. P.T.L. has been in business since 1929 as an intraprovincial Ontario carrier. *Doug Grieve*

Hauling produce to market from Florida before it spoils requires equipment that will keep moving to get the job done. Over the years, Greenstein Trucking Co. of Pompano Beach, Florida, has had a fleet of trucks that kept freight moving and making deliveries. During the 1980s, this LTL 9000 Ford tractor and Great Dane reefer trailer was one of the nice units of equipment in the fleet. Greenstein has been hauling refrigerated products since 1961. *Harry Patterson*

Hauling building materials, granite construction materials, and general freight requires a variety of trailers. Anderson Trucking Service, Inc. of St. Cloud, Minnesota, has authority to haul the above-mentioned commodities across the United States with 16 terminals spread around the country. A fleet of 900 tractors and 2,160 trailers deliver the loads for Anderson customers. Owner-operator tractors make up about half the fleet, like this Peterbilt 379 tractor decked out with chrome and a fancy paint job, which is pulling a Strick trailer. *Neil Sherff*

The Canadian companies had tractor-trailer rigs that were different from what we had here in the United States. A common type of unit that both the states and Canada had was double trailers. Motorways, Ltd. (formerly Soo-Security Motorways, Ltd.) of Winnipeg, Manitoba, ran these kinds of double trailers. The unit shown here is an L9000 Ford tractor with Trailmobile trailers. A fleet of 246 tractors and 960 trailers covered an area from Montreal, Quebec, to the Canadian Pacific Coast. *Doug Grieve*

With better fuel mileage a priority in the late 1970s and early 1980s, aerodynamics began to influence truck design. Nose-cone fronts for trailers came first, followed by changes by the tractor manufacturers. Preston Trucking Co., Inc. of Preston, Maryland, came up with its own wind-cheating cab design using a GMC Brigadier tractor equipped with a Caterpillar 3406 Diesel Engine getting 7.63 miles per gallon in an economy challenge pulling two Budd 27-foot trailers. Preston began in 1932 and in 1990 had a fleet of more than 2,200 tractors and 5,700 trailers covering an area from Illinois to Massachusetts. *Preston Trucking Co., Inc.*

Hauling produce from California to the East Coast without spoilage meant that once the truck was loaded, it had to constantly keep moving. C. R. England and Sons, Inc. of Salt Lake City, Utah, was a big hauler of produce from west to east and got the cargo to markets in fine shape. For many years, Kenworth trucks were the power source with a few International Emeryvilles. In recent years, Freightliner tractors pull the Utility reefer trailers. England has been giving dedicated service to its customers since 1946. *Harry Patterson*

Watkins Motor Lines, Inc. of Lakeland, Florida, started in the hauling business in 1932. In ensuing years, Watkins hauled produce and reefers, but it changed to general freight. In the 1960s, two Watkins divisions were Watkins Carolina Express, Inc. and Watkins Texas Express, Inc. Both were run with owner-operators. Around 1990 there were a total of 1,230 tractors and more than 2,800 trailers. The Kenworth tractor and Great Dane trailers create a good image for the company. *Watkins Motor Lines, Inc.*

Over the course of trucking history, a lot of carriers tried to be dedicated to one make of truck. But when purchasing a new fleet, the best deals always win. C W Transport Co. of Wisconsin Rapids, Wisconsin, had a mixed fleet. GMC, Whites, and White-Freightliners were three of the known brands they had over the years. Shown here is an early-1980s GMC Brigadier pulling a matching set of double Trailmobile trailers. The fleet totaled 366 tractors and 1,080 trailers covering a 13-state area. *C W Transport Co.*

Since the early 1930s, many trucking companies have come and gone. Those who survived typically did so by expanding their operations. However, there were those who remained within their original regions, such as Ward Trucking Corp. of Altoona, Pennsylvania. Ward was a Pennsylvania and New Jersey carrier with eight terminals. This GMC General and Fruehauf trailer is part of a fleet of 250 tractors and 431 trailers. *Ward Trucking Co., Inc.*

It is rare today to see a truck as colorful as those of St. Germain Transport, Ltd. of St. Germain, Canada. The company is classified as a general freight hauler covering Canada and the United States. It has a variety of different brands of trucks in its fleet. This colorful T-600 Kenworth tractor is an eye-catcher, along with matched graphics on a Trailmobile trailer. *Ron Adams collection*

Many of the household goods carriers had trucks in their fleet equipped with a Dromedary body, since household goods are often light freight. Paul Arpin Van Lines, Inc. of East Greenwich, Rhode Island, used Dromedary bodies on some of its rigs to maximize the gross weight of these light loads. The International tractor is set to haul the Matlock trailer. *Harry Patterson*

Back in the good old days of trucking in the 1940s and 1950s, if a truck had a few extra pieces of chrome, a two-color paint job, and a few extra lights, it was considered a really nice truck. But when you compare a truck like that to a truck like this W-900 Kenworth, you know it must be the 1990s. Global Van Lines, Inc. of Orange, California, most likely feels proud to have a truck like this in its fleet. It not only makes a good impression on the company, but shows driver pride as well. *Neil Sherff*

Back in the 1930s, trucking companies were usually one-man operations. But Bender & Loudon Motor Freight, Inc. of Akron, Ohio, was a two-man partnership. Throughout the company's history, 23 terminals were established with a total of approximately 250 tractors and 450 trailers in the fleet. One of those units is this White tractor and Fruehauf trailer. *Bender & Loudon Motor Freight, Inc.*

Most of the Canadian rigs are somewhat different than those in the United States. Axle spread and B train rigs are two differences (see page 300 for B train). In this case, this looks like a typical American over-the-road truck, but it belongs to Day & Ross, Ltd. of Canada. For many years, its orange-and-black trucks have been a familiar sight on the Canadian and American highways. The Freightliner shows the pride that Day & Ross, Ltd. has for its equipment. *Dick Copello*

Swinging beef, frozen meat, seafood, and frozen foods are the main cargo hauled in reefer trailers. Dry freight can also be hauled at times on a return trip. Refrigerated Food Express of Boston was one successful heavy user of reefer trailers. Its territory stretched from New England to the Midwest. The W-900 Kenworth tractor and Utility reefer trailer made the deliveries on time. *Dick Copello*

So often, we hear the saying "Like father, like son." This seems to apply in this case. SGT 2000, Inc. and St. Germain Transport are a father-and-son operation. SGT 2000, Inc. is owned by the father with about 300 tractors and trailers. St. Germain Transport, Ltd. is owned by the son and has about 50 tractors and trailers. This sharp-looking W-900 Kenworth with matching flatbed trailer is one of the son's. Both companies haul coast to coast in Canada, the United States, and down to Mexico. Both are located on the same lot and share both garage and dock facilities. *Francois Spenard*

APPENDIX

Magazines

Wheels of Time
P.O. Box 531168
Birmingham, AL 35253-1168

Overdrive Magazine
P.O. Box 3187
Tuscaloosa, AL 35403-9870

Commercial Car Journal
P.O. Box 7670
Highlands Ranch, CO 80163-7670

Fleet Owner
11 Riverbend Rd, South
Stamford, CT 0607-0211

Truckers New Magazine
P.O. Box 3187
Tuscaloosa, AL 35403-9838

Owner Operator
201 King of Prussia Road
Radnor, PA 19089

Heavy Duty Trucking
38 Executive Park, Suite 300
Irvine, CA 92614

INDEX

316